M000117484

# THE LIFE & MUSIC
## OF HARRY STYLES
### UNOFFICIAL & UNAUTHORIZED

Published by Mortimer
An imprint of Welbeck Non-Fiction Limited,
part of Welbeck Publishing Group.
Based in London and Sydney.

Copyright 2018, 2022 © Welbeck Publishing Group Limited

Disclaimer: All trademarks, copyright, quotations, company names,
registered names, products, characters, logos and catchphrases used
or cited in this book are the property of their respective owners. This
book is a publication of Mortimer, an imprint of Welbeck Publishing
Group Limited, and has not been licensed, approved, sponsored, or
endorsed by any person or entity.

All rights reserved. This book is sold subject to the condition that it
may not be reproduced, stored in a retrieval system or transmitted
in any form or by any means, electronic, mechanical, photocopying,
recording or otherwise, without the publisher's prior consent.

A CIP catalogue for this book is available from the British Library.

ISBN 978-1-83861-150-7

10 9 8 7 6 5 4 3 2 1

Printed and bound in Dubai

# THE LIFE & MUSIC OF HARRY STYLES

### UNOFFICIAL & UNAUTHORIZED

**MALCOLM CROFT**

MORTIMER

# Contents

# Introduction
## HARRY'S WORLD

HARRY STYLES IS THE BIGGEST STAR IN THE WORLD. FROM *THE X FACTOR* TO ONE DIRECTION, HOLMES CHAPEL TO HOLLYWOOD (VIA *DUNKIRK* AND *DON'T WORRY DARLING*), THIS MULTI-TALENTED SINGER-SONGWRITER, ACTOR, FASHION ICON AND A-LIST CELEBRITY IS ON A PATH TO BECOMING A RENAISSANCE MAN OF THE TWENTY-FIRST CENTURY – BEFORE HE EVEN CELEBRATES HIS 30TH BIRTHDAY. HE'S ALREADY CLOCKED UP THREE AWESOME ALBUMS AND HAS THE WORLD AT HIS FEET AS HE TOURS THE GLOBE TO PACKED STADIUMS. LONG MAY HE REIGN...

Perhaps not since Elvis Presley has one man made such an impact wherever he goes. Perhaps not since the Beatles has one musician made such a beautiful noise in a band that genuinely changed the world. And while, of course, there will be in the years to come other superstars eager to steal the crown from Harry Styles' immaculate bonce, for now, right now, today, this is Harry Styles' moment in the sun. And it isn't just a fleeting 15 minutes of fame, as many predicted in 2010. Harry has ascended to his position as the true prince of rock and pop – and he is here to stay. While many of his pop contemporaries have fallen by the wayside, unable to sustain their fame, going off the rails, or succumbing to lurid controversy, Harry has furrowed his own quiet path, buoyed by a sensible head on his shoulders and a tightknit group of family, friends and musicians who help keep him on the straight and narrow, and aiming for the prize for which he so seriously yearns – global success through honesty and awesome tunes, achieved without compromise. Harry has accomplished all of this without selling his soul to the highest bidder. He has remained honest in the face of adversity; he has remained kind in the face of treachery; he has remained energetic in the face of severe exhaustion – and he has remained himself when so much fame and fortune might have persuaded him to change everything about who he is.

To this day, the real Harry Styles remains a mystery, and his fans, it seems, are quite happy to forever be chasing the truth about this century's first global mega icon. The truth, however, is that no one will ever know the real Harry Styles because, to quote the man himself, "that mystery... it's just what I like."

**Left:** Harry shows off his short hair at the *Dunkirk* world premiere in London, July 13, 2017.

# Chapter One

## THE BOY WHO WOULD BE KING

# THE BOY WHO WOULD BE KING

IT ALMOST SEEMS LIKE YESTERDAY SINCE HARRY STYLES WALKED ONTO THE STAGE OF THE X FACTOR FOR SERIES SEVEN OF THE GLOBAL TV PHENOMENON. THAT WAS 2010. IN THE YEARS SINCE, HARRY – DESCRIBED BY HIS FORMER 1D BANDMATES, AND EVERYONE WHO HAS EVER MET HIM, AS SOMEONE "BORN TO BE A ROCK STAR" – HAS BECOME A GLOBAL ICON. THIS IS HIS STORY.

Born on a Tuesday afternoon, Harry Edward Styles was welcomed into the world via Worcestershire. As a baby, his family moved to a beautiful village in Cheshire. "It's quite boring, nothing much ever happens there. It's quite picturesque," Harry claimed in his audition segment for *The X Factor*, with a cheeky smile. Of course, and somewhat ironically, the village is now famous for being anything but boring as the Home of Harry Styles.

His big sister, Gemma, adored him from day one. The feeling was mutual, and Harry would later claim that she was the "smart one". In 2017, Gemma, a freelance writer on technology and millennial trends, wrote an article for *Another Man* magazine in which she remembered a family holiday to Cyprus with then seven-year-old Harry. "He was holding court around the pool with people three times his age. When he left on a shuttle bus back to the airport ... there was a crowd of young, adult women gathered on the pavement waving him off through the window, shouting their goodbyes." It seems that from even the youngest of ages, Harry was destined to be a star. "When I was little I knew that I wanted to entertain people. I was a proper show-off," Harry himself has admitted, adding: "I could always hear my sister's music and I used to pretend to have a guitar and, like, perform in my mirror in my bedroom."

**Left:** Harry attends a press conference ahead of *The X-Factor* final at The Connaught Hotel, December 9, 2010.

**Above:** Harry and sister Gemma Styles attend the *Another Man* London launch event hosted by Harry, October 6, 2016.

"Unlike Holmes Chapel, pretty much every other part of my life has changed, apart from like coming down here; it's exactly the same."

Harry's father was a huge fan of classic rock, and the Rolling Stones, Pink Floyd, Fleetwood Mac and Queen formed a musical education that young Harry absorbed into his bloodstream. Indeed, his debut solo album, *Harry Styles*, shows how much rock has taken hold of his spirit and soul. Indeed, Harry remembers bouncing around to *The Dark Side of the Moon*, the seminal album by prog rockers Pink Floyd, before he could even walk. "I couldn't really get it," Harry remembers, "but I just remember being like – *this is really fucking cool*. Then my mom would always have Shania Twain, and Savage Garden, Norah Jones going on. I had a great childhood. I'll admit it."

If Harry's rock style was gifted to him by his dad, then it was his mum who gave him his keen ear for pop melodies, especially after his parents split up. About that he has said: "That was quite a weird time. I remember crying about it. I didn't really get what was going on properly, I was just sad that my parents wouldn't be together anymore. I'm lucky in that I never had to do that thing of experiencing divided loyalties when they split up. Feeling loved and supported by them never changed during that. Honestly, when

you're that young, you can kind of block it out … I can't say that I remember the exact thing. I didn't realize that was the case until just now. Yeah, I mean, I was seven. It's one of those things. Feeling supported and loved by my parents never changed."

Harry's sadness at his parents' divorce was replaced by living in a house where positivity and strength overcame any obstacle. Proof of this, and the impact of his mother Anne, comes from Harry himself, who has said: "My mom is very strong. She has the greatest heart. Her house in Cheshire is where I go when I want to spend some me time."

**Left:** As featured in 2014's *This Is US*, Harry's childhood home in Holmes Chapel, Cheshire.

**Above, Left:** Harry with his mum, Anne Cox, at Sony Music's post-BRITs party at the Arts Club, London, February 20, 2013.

**Above, Right:** Harry returns home to Chestnut Drive, Holmes Chapel during the filming of *This Is Us*, 2014.

Indeed, it was Anne, and Harry's bond with his family, that kept him sane through the early years of madness and fame. "She's never made me feel like I have to prove myself," Harry said of her. "A lot of people grow up not really talking about how they feel about each other, but our house is always filled with loving each other." Harry's love for his mum, and his sister, was highlighted by his close friend and TV producer, Ben Winston, who housed and fed the young star in the attic of his house in London for the first two years of One Direction, offering Harry a familial sanctuary away from the noise of fame. Asked in a 2017 interview what matters most to Harry, Ben Winston had one answer: "Family. It comes from his mom, Anne. She brought him and his sister up incredibly well. Harry would choose boring over exciting ... There is more chance of me going to Mars next week than there is of Harry having some sort of addiction."

Despite all the flamboyant fashions and prankster antics, Harry yearns to be normal. In Morgan Spurlock's 2013 documentary *One Direction: This Is Us*, with the now famous scenes of the boys back home in their respective family houses, each band member cries out for the word "normal". For Harry, normal was going back to Mum's house, "... where there's tea on the table. When you've been away you appreciate it so much more. I think the best part of having time off is whenever I go home to my parents' house, I usually fall asleep on the sofa for three hours, and you don't have to set an alarm. It's just nice to go home and do the really normal things that you didn't appreciate as much before, like sitting and having a meal with your family is so nice. You behave for your parents and do all of your chores."

Ironically, this concept of wanting to appear "normal" is what made One Direction even more famous, and therefore abnormal. "I don't know why the girls love us so much," said Harry in 2012. "I think it's because we don't pretend to be anything we're not. Yes, we can be idiots at times. We're like those boys in the back of class throwing paper and making a noise. I think girls can relate to us in that classroom way; we're just normal lads." Niall agreed: "This is actually what we are. We're just normal.

**Left:** Harry poses with his fans outside his home in Holmes Chapel, 2014.

We are not doing anything different, that's what I mean by also being normal, our job just happened to be abnormal." When pictured holding hands with Taylor Swift in New York's Central Park in 2012, it was Harry who wished that there were no paparazzi, no onlookers, no cameras – nothing "glitzy". All those other people ruined the normality he so desperately craved, especially when on a date with a girl he fancied. This walk in the park with one of the world's most famous songwriters is now something he is asked about all the time, and something which he still thinks about.

As Harry star's rose, sometime around early 2011, and as the routine of superstardom started to kick in, Harry did something that many of his contemporaries would never have done. Rather than buying a multi-million-pound house, Harry decided to go live in an attic, on a spare mattress, at a mate's house. For 20 months. From today's perspective, that time living

a "normal" life, which was kept a secret until 2017, may be what saved Harry from going off the rails. In an interview in 2017, Ben Winston said: "Those 20 months were when they went from being on a reality show, *X Factor*, to being the biggest-selling artists in the world – that period of time, Harry was living with us in the most mundane suburban situation. No one ever found out, really. Even when we went out for a meal, it's such a sweet family neighbourhood, no one dreamed it was actually him. But he made our house a home. And when he moved out, we were gutted."

However, Harry's time at the Winston family home in North London was not without its funny anecdotes. Harry was still the biggest star in the world, after all; he was allowed some excesses! "My wife, Meri, and I, we had this joke," Ben Winston recalled. "Meri and I would like to see the girls that he would come back with to the house. That was always what we enjoyed, because we'd be in bed like an old couple.

# "I had a really nice upbringing. I feel very lucky. I had a great family and always felt loved. There's nothing worse than an inauthentic tortured person."

We'd have our spot cream on our faces and we'd be in our pyjamas and the door would go off. The stairwell was right outside our door, so we'd wait to see if Harry was coming home alone or with people."

"I was alone," Styles insisted. "I was scared of Meri."

"He wasn't always alone," Winston corrected, "but it was exciting seeing the array of A-listers that would come up and sleep in the attic. Or they'd come and lounge with us. We'd never discuss business. He would act as if he hadn't come back from playing to 80,000 people three nights in a row in Rio de Janeiro."

With fame, success and money – not to mention playing to 80,000 screaming fans (predominantly girls) every night – starting to take its toll ("You're never going to get used to walking into a room and have people screaming at you," Harry has claimed), it's easy to believe that Harry took plenty of girls back to his attic.

**Left:** As *X Factor* finalists, Zayn, Harry, Louis, Liam and Niall smile for cameras at Fountain Studios, London, November 12, 2010.

**Right:** Harry and Louis behind-the-scenes at the *X Factor* studios, December 12, 2010.

Though, according to the singer himself, this is inaccurate: "Quite a lot of the girls I get photographed with are just friends and then, according to the papers, I have, like, 7,000 girlfriends." While he has, no doubt, been luckier than most in this department, it appears that Harry has more respect for the opposite sex than some contemporaries in his position. "A lot of the time, the way it's portrayed is that I only see women in a sexual way. I grew up with just my mum and sister, so I respect women a lot," Harry has commented, when asked about the notches on his bedpost – or lack thereof. Harry's honesty about his sexuality, and his relationships with girls (famous or not), has highlighted just how different Harry is from other pop stars, who have either exploited or taken advantage of their fame.

Characteristically, perhaps, Harry doesn't see all of this as a big deal. "I've never felt the need to explain myself in terms of my personal life," Harry said in 2017, hoping that now, as a mature solo artist,

he would not have to answer questions about his love life again. Of course, wherever Harry goes, sensationalist tabloid rumours will always follow him around; it's the nature of the beast. The fact, though, that most One Direction members have close relationships with their older sisters (Liam has two, Zayn has three, Harry has one, and Louis has four half-sisters) does explain why "normal" Harry and the rest of the "normal" bandmates were able to relate so well to girls, and girl fans. It can also be said that having sisters also bound the boys together, each of them finding in the others the brothers they never had – yet another detail that explains why these five particular boys had such powerful chemistry.

**Above:** One Direction performing at G-A-Y Heaven nightclub, London, September 17, 2011.

**Right:** Harry living the high life on a private plane ... while checking in with his millions of fans on his Twitter account.

"

That's the amazing thing about music, there's a song for every emotion. Can you imagine a world with no music? It would suck and I'd still be a baker.

"

Of course, Harry did have girlfriends as a teenager, and before he first auditioned on *The X Factor* in 2010. His first girlfriend was called Abigail: "My first proper girlfriend used to have one of those laughs. There was also a little bit of mystery with her because she didn't go to our school. I just worshipped the ground she walked on. And she knew, probably to a fault, a little. That was a tough one. I was 15. She used to live an hour and a half away on the train, and I worked in a bakery for three years. I'd finish on Saturdays at 4.30 and it was a 4.42 train, and if I missed it there wasn't one for another hour or two. So, I'd finish and sprint to the train station. Spent 70 per cent of my wages on train tickets. Later, I'd remember her perfume. Little things. I smell that perfume all the time. I'll be in a lift or a reception and say to someone, 'Alien, right?' And sometimes they're impressed and sometimes they're a little creeped out. 'Stop smelling me.'"

Working at the bakery in Holmes Chapel was his first job, which he began at the age of 14. Fans of Morgan Spurlock's documentary will remember the bakery as one of the highlights of the film, with Harry returning to the bakery and reuniting with his former colleagues. "I worked at a bakery for a couple of years. I worked for the old ladies. Very nice old ladies," he quipped to the camera. The local bakery may have prepared Harry for the rigours and routine of touring and life on the road with 1D: every Saturday he would wake up at 5 a.m. and walk to the bakery to do his day shift of selling bread to the village's residents. During this age, Harry visited a careers councillor at school and remembers being unsure of what he wanted to do with his life. For a while he thought he wanted to be a physiotherapist, but then: "We had a workshop at school where we went in to talk about what we wanted to do and essentially someone told me there were no jobs in that, so I should pick something else. I was a little stumped, to be honest."

**Above:** One Direction perform at Carphone Warehouse on London's Oxford Street, October 12, 2011.

"I always said, at the very beginning, all I wanted was to be the granddad with the best stories … and the best shelf of artefacts and bits and trinkets."

While working his Saturday shift at the bakery, Harry began to grow ambitions of studying law and perhaps becoming a lawyer. A rock and roll lawyer, no doubt! But those early aspirations were put to bed when Harry joined his first band, White Eskimo. The band are still going strong in 2017, despite losing their lead singer to One Direction, the biggest pop band of all time. YouTube has many videos of Harry and White Eskimo practising, which are well worth checking out. You'll see Harry's pure talent shine through. "We wrote a couple of songs," Harry remembers about this former group. "One was called 'Gone in a Week'. It was about luggage. *I'll be gone in a week or two/ Trying to find myself someplace new/ I don't need any jackets or shoes/ The only luggage I need is you.*"

Harry's time in White Eskimo was instrumental in Harry's desire to turn away from the law books and concentrate on rock and roll. "I sing in a band with some friends from school," Harry proudly first told Dermot O'Leary during his audition segment for *The X Factor*. "I'm the lead singer. We entered the Battle of the Bands competition, and we won. Winning that competition and playing in front of lots of people made me realize that that is what I want to do. I got such a thrill when I was singing in front of people it made me want to do more and more." In another interview, Harry recalled how performing with White Eskimo gave him the confidence to perform in front of people, as well as something to tell his career counsellor the time next they met. For it was then that he decided he didn't want to be a baker, or lawyer, or physiotherapist – he wanted to be a musician. A serious musician. "I remember how nervous I was before we performed a gig," Harry said of White Eskimo, "but then afterwards, that feeling about everyone watching you do something that you were enjoying really resonated with me. That adrenaline rush I like."

Of course, Harry left White Eskimo the very minute he got through the first round of the *The X Factor* and had taken the first step to pursue his dream of becoming a breakthrough solo artist. Though, as we know, it would only be a matter of just two months before Harry would become a member of yet another band. A band heading in only one direction.

**Above:** The boys go dressed to impress at the *GQ* Style Awards, 2010.

**Left:** Proud mentor Simon Cowell praises his protegeés at a press conference ahead of *The X-Factor* final, December 9, 2010.

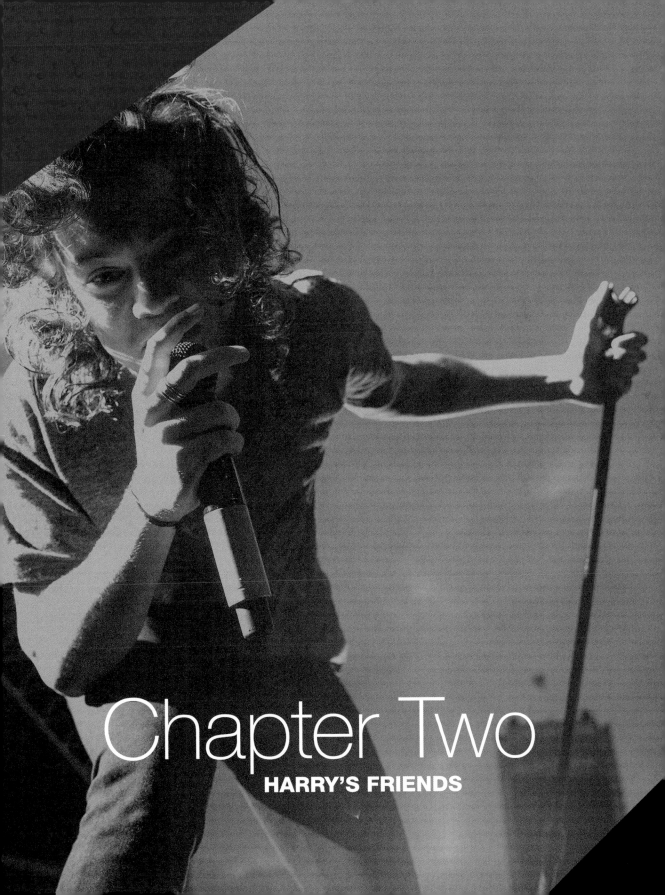

# Chapter Two
## HARRY'S FRIENDS

# HARRY'S FRIENDS

WITH MORE THAN 30 MILLION FOLLOWERS ON TWITTER, AND MORE THAN 150 MILLION VIEWS OF 'SIGN OF THE TIMES' ON YOUTUBE, HARRY STYLES ISN'T SHORT ON FRIENDS OR FANS. HOWEVER, OVER THE PAST FEW YEARS, HE HAS BECOME FAMOUS FOR HIS FAMOUS FRIENDS AND GIRLFRIENDS, ENSURING THAT HARRY REMAINS IN THE ZOOM LENS OF PAPARAZZI EVERYWHERE HE GOES.

## ED SHEERAN

One Direction songwriter ('Little Things', '18', 'Moments' and 'Over Again') and close friend to the band, Ed shares a few friendship tattoos with Harry, too – the Pingu tattoo being the most memorable. In 2015, Ed said that he no longer needed to write songs for One Direction, as they had become too good at song writing themselves.

## TAYLOR SWIFT

Harry's three-month "friendship" seemed too good to be true – the World's Biggest Female Artist and the World's Hottest Male Artist hooking up for love. Harry has remained tight-lipped on Tay-Tay, saying about their famous second date in New York's Central Park: "When I see photos from that day I think relationships are hard, at any age. And adding in that you don't really understand exactly how it works when you're 18, trying to navigate all that stuff didn't make it easier. I mean, you're a little bit awkward to begin with. You're on a date with someone you really like. It should be that simple, right? It was a learning experience for sure. But at the heart of it – I just wanted it to be a normal date."

**Above:** Ed and Harry attend the 2013 Teen Choice Awards at Gibson Amphitheatre, Los Angeles, August 11.

**Right:** The picture seen around the world. Swift-Styles in New York's Central Park, December 2, 2012.

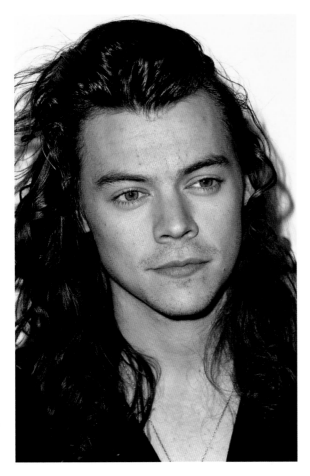

## BEN WINSTON

Twelve years Harry's senior, TV producer Ben Winston let Harry sleep upstairs in his attic for the first 20 months of Harry's fame. It was living with Ben and his wife Meri that kept Harry's feet on the ground, as his world started spinning out of control.

## JAMES CORDEN

Ben is James' producer, and the trio of Ben, Harry and James have been friends since Ben first filmed the band's music videos 'Best Song Ever', 'Story of My Life', 'Midnight Memories' and 'You & I'. Harry took up a week-long residency on *The Late Late Show with James Corden* to promote his debut album Harry Styles in June 2017. "Harry was at my wedding, and I love him absolutely dearly, and I'm so proud," said Corden. "I don't give him any love advice, are you joking? It's a miracle we're technically the same species. He needs no advice from me. He knows what he's doing in all facets of his life."

## NICK GRIMSHAW

BBC Radio One's highly successful *Breakfast Show* presenter, Nick 'Grimmie' Grimshaw has been a firm favourite since 1D's earliest days. The pair were, for a time, joined at the hip. "It seems totally normal to me," Nick said about Harry, "a DJ being mates with a pop star. It's not like he's some weirdo who can't talk. He's really funny. When anyone meets him, it's like, 'Oh yeah, he's really nice and interesting.'"

**Left:** Harry and good friend, James Corden, go for dinner at London's swanky Sketch restaurant, January 9, 2013.

**Above, Left:** Harry snapped arriving at KIIS FM's Jingle Ball in Los Angeles, California, December 4, 2015.

**Above, Right:** Harry and Grimmie celebrate the launch of the Nick Grimshaw for TOPMAN fashion collection, Odette's Primrose Hill, London, June 4, 2015.

### KENDALL JENNER

"She's a huge part of the album," stated Harry, about his debut album. Many believe this statement to be about Kendall Jenner, Harry's friend since 2013, when the two went on a Caribbean cruise together. "Sometimes you want to tip the hat, and sometimes you just want to give them the whole cap ... and hope they know it's just for them."

### CAROLINE FLACK

Fourteen years older than Harry, the *X Factor* presenter received some flak for dating Harry when he was 17. The pair ended their brief relationship in January 2012.

### DAVID BECKHAM

Who doesn't want to be friends with David Beckham?

### ZACH BRAFF

The *Scrubs* TV star and Harry became friends in 2014. "I don't really know how we know each other, we just got in touch. I'm a big fan," Harry said. Zach replied in kind: "For those of you asking, Harry Styles is a dynamite singer."

---

**Above:** David Beckham and Harry share a cuddle at a movie premiere, December 1, 2013.

**Right:** Harry and new BFF Zach Braff attend the premiere of Braff's 'Wish I Was Here' at the Marc Theatre during the 2014 Sundance Film Festival, Utah, January 18.

## CAMILLE ROWE

As of mid-July 2017, Harry's current girlfriend is Victoria's Secret model and actress Camille Rowe . Four years older than Harry, the French-American seems to be smitten – and apparently the feeling is mutual. When Nick Grimshaw submitted Harry to his BBC *Breakfast Show*'s 'Heart Rate Challenge', Harry was presented with a picture of Rowe. "I don't know her. I'm sure she's a wonderful person," Harry replied very unconvincingly.

## CARA DELEVINGNE

Best friends since 2011, Harry and supermodel Cara seemed for a long time to be perfect for each other – both respectively at the top of their games. Despite Harry frequently stating, "She's not my girl!" the two were often seen together in public supporting each other's careers. He once told the media that Cara was "very good at walking" down the catwalk.

**Right:** Cara Delevingne, Clara Paget and Harry party during London Fashion Week, September 21, 2015.

**Overleaf:** Catherine, Duchess of Cambridge meets Harry at the Royal Variety Performance, London Palladium, November 13, 2014.

"Harry has loads of secret celebrity phone numbers and we find out about them later. We'll see something in the papers and be like: 'What's going on here?' and he'll be like: 'Oh, it's Gary from Take That or whoever, don't worry about it.'

LIAM PAYNE

**Left:** One Direction's final live show, Sheffield Arena, October 31, 2015.

# Chapter Three

**THE X FACTOR**

# THE X FACTOR

FROM THE MOMENT HARRY WALKED OUT ON THE MANCHESTER CENTRAL ARENA OF THE X FACTOR STAGE ON APRIL 11, 2010, IT WAS OBVIOUS THAT THIS YOUNG MAN HAD SOMETHING EXTRA SPECIAL ABOUT HIM. HE HAD STAR POWER, FOR SURE. HE HAD THAT X FACTOR. NO ARTIST BEFORE HIM, SAVE LEONA LEWIS PERHAPS, HAD ALL THE MAGIC INGREDIENTS THAT SIMON COWELL AND CO. WERE LOOKING FOR. HOWEVER, HARRY'S DREAM OF BECOMING A SOLO SINGING STAR DIDN'T QUITE GO TO PLAN. AT LEAST, NOT STRAIGHTAWAY...

The course of true love never did run smooth, as William Shakespeare once wrote. Harry's love of singing, and his dreams of becoming a solo artist, deviated from the expected path after his first audition in front of the judges: Simon Cowell, Louis Walsh, Cheryl Cole and Dannii Minogue. After his less than impressive performance in the Bootcamp section of the show, it was Nicole Scherzinger, a guest judge, who suggested to Simon Cowell that Harry team up with four other talented young men – each of them too good to let go, but not good enough to stand alone.

**Left:** The band bond backstage at the Patriot Centre, Virginia, March 2, 2012.

"

I think, you know, we entered the *The X Factor* in the UK, and you kind of want someone who knows what they're talking about to tell you if you're any good or not instead of just your mum saying that she likes it when you sing.

"

# "I'm Harry Styles, I'm sixteen and I'm from Holmes Chapel in Cheshire."

They had all made glorious first impressions, but at quite young ages they didn't quite have the confidence to be solo artists in their own right.

"I think, you know, we entered *The X Factor* in the UK, and you kind of want someone who knows what they're talking about to tell you if you're any good or not instead of just your mum saying that she likes it when you sing," Harry remembered of the time. As is often the case in the world of pop, mums play a vital role in encouragement. Sometimes a mother's faith can be misplaced, but Harry's mum, Anne, knew that her son had the X factor. It was she who had suggested Harry give the Boys category of *The X Factor* 2010 a shot, after watching him take a firm interest in singing with his local band White Eskimo – and, obviously, hearing him sing in the shower at home around the house.

When asked onstage about himself by Simon Cowell, Harry replied: "Erm, I work in a bakery. I work there on Saturdays." And when quizzed further by Simon about why he was there Harry replied: "I've always wanted to audition, but I've always been too young." There were squeals of affection from the crowd.

Singing Stevie Wonder's romantic pop ballad 'Isn't She Lovely', Harry received a positive response from Nicole, but Louis Walsh's takedown of Harry has now become infamous: "I think you're still too young. I don't think you have enough experience or confidence just yet." Thankfully, Simon was on hand to deliver the honest truth to Louis with just one word: "Rubbish." Simon and Nicole gave Harry two yeses and sent the singer through to the next round of the competition. But that was was only the beginning, as Harry observed: "In that instant, you're in the whirlwind.

**Above:** Harry performs with 1D at Z100's Jingle Ball, New York, December 7, 2012.

**Overleaf:** 1D wows the *The X Factor US*, during the Live Elimination Show, Los Angeles, November 8, 2012.

You don't really know what's happening; you're just a kid on the show. You don't even know you're good at anything. I'd gone because my mum told me I was good from singing in the car ... but your mum tells you things to make you feel good, so you take it with a pinch of salt. I didn't really know what I was expecting when I went on there." Thankfully, Harry's faith in himself, and his mum's, won the day and Harry's dream of finding fortune as a solo singer came true. Sort of ...

In July 2010, guest judge Nicole Scherzinger insisted that the male teenagers from the 'Boys' category – Louis Tomlinson, Liam Payne, Niall Horan, Zayn Malik and Harry Styles – were simply too good to jettison from the competition. The five-piece band was put together. "I made a decision and I did it in about 10 minutes, why don't we put those five boys into a group?" said Simon Cowell.

One Direction – or 1D, whichever you prefer – went on to conquer the world from this very show despite not winning the competition or even coming second, and despite being a group of five boys who had not met before or sung together before, and who were unsure if they even liked each other. Each of the five boys had individual good looks, charm and talent, but the odds of success as a group were against them. But for each of them, it was One Direction or bust. The rest is history, we know now. But let's slow things down. Between 2010 and 2015, One Direction reached the topmost peaks of popmost perfection. But it wasn't all easy-going, as the band have recounted in many of their earliest interviews.

"Before we got together as a band," Zayn claimed, "we were kind of each other's competition because we're from the same category on X Factor. But as soon as we got put together we all got on really well. We all went to Harry's place and stayed there together to get to know each other."

When we first got together we went to Wembley to see Take That and we thought, 'Yeah that's what we want to be doing.' Fifteen years from now we want One Direction to be playing a gig together at Wembley. The tickets aren't available yet, but hold on, because one day they will be …

**Left:** One Direction perform onstage.

In a separate interview, Louis disagreed at first – "We used to be at each other's throats while we were on *The X Factor!*" – before admitting, "but we had similar ambitions, similar goals. I suppose that's why we got on together." Harry, forever the sensible one, recalled this crazy time in his life perfectly. "We were all going through this new experience, we all kind of entered it in the same mindset. It was like we were all starting school."

In a poignant and revealing interview for *Teen Vogue* with Maude Apatow, the daughter of film director Judd Apatow, the boys opened up (very rare back in those days) about those early days as members of One Direction. Zayn commented: "When we were on *The X Factor*, we didn't realize how overnight the fame thing was. We didn't really understand it until we went on a shopping trip. It was like Week 7 or 8 of the show. We went with a few other contestants and there were loads of people, packed. Our parents are obviously proud, but they're still trying to get used to the fact that we're in a band. I have a feeling my mom would actually like One Direction if I wasn't in it!"

Harry chimed in: "Our families always come and support us. This is all happening, yet our families keep us grounded. I think we try just as hard as we can to just be ourselves. I think that is important especially with the way the world is at the moment. There are so many things telling people to be other than themselves. We try to be who we are while not being stupid."

All of the boys have claimed at various times they "hated" being in the band, in part because immense success for 1D came with overwhelming fame. Due to their humble and strong family-orientated backgrounds, this has never sat easily with any of the members of the band. For One Direction "fame" is an ugly word.

**Above:** Harry poses with his fans at the 2012 MTV Video Music Awards, September 6.

**Right:** The "Classic" Harry pose, 2012 MTV Video Music Awards, September 6.

"You know like people saying 'you're famous", it just gives you no substance. It's not like 'He's a really nice guy' or 'He's really funny'; it like becomes this thing, like 'You're famous'. It's just like weird, I hate it. One of the reasons why I do not like the word 'famous' [is] because then people use it afterwards, and they go like 'You used to be famous' or 'He's not famous anymore' and just like, this is weird," said Harry, who as de facto leader of the band shouldered an additional degree of fame. Some of this he attracted himself by courting it in his extracurricular activities, and some of it was thrust upon him – because, according to first Zayn and then Liam, "Harry is the perfect pop star. Just born for it, like loves it," and "Harry, he just likes to go out and have a good time, does not want to waste the moment."

With so much fame at their fingertips, it is surprising that none of the members of the band have gone off the rails. The band has yet to succumb to a career-damaging controversy. This is down to the love they receive from their honest fans and their mums. For Harry's mum, Anne, her son's fame brought anxiety. "It takes a bit of getting used to, it feels quite surreal," she said when Harry first made the headlines. "You

sort of feel so proud, you feel like your heart could burst sometimes, but in the back of your mind, there's always that bit of feeling that, you got to be kind of ready to pick up the pieces if, if it stops."

"I actually think that the kind of fans that we've had are the most honest," said Harry when asked about the band's success and their ability to stay level-headed despite all the chaos. Simon Cowell agreed: "To me, once they left the show, it was all about the fans, literally, from the second they finished, the fans made it their mission that One Direction was going become the biggest band in the world." In the early days, en route to becoming the world's most famous five teenagers, each member of 1D expressed countless thanks and appreciation to the people who made them the stars they are. It is this sincere gratitude for their loyal and dedicated fan base that kept the group strong and united, especially when faced with exhaustion and adversity. "The fans completely changed our lives. Even when you're having a bad day, the energy of 50,000 screaming fans is what lifts you. You can't go out on stage with a scowl. They keep us going. Out of all the success we

have had, the fact that we have been put in a position to do something tangible for our fans is the best thing we have achieved so far."

In Morgan Spurlock's documentary, *This Is Us*, several Directioners had the opportunity to speak to the camera and tell the world their feelings about their favourite band. "We love them because they sing our feelings", "They make us believe that everything is possible if we believe in our self." The band's ability to make their fans feel good about themselves made them seem like the genuine article, the real deal – and the fans have shown their appreciation. "I honestly think they'll write books about One Direction fans," Louis said. "Because they are so fanatical. The intensity. It's remarkable." Simon Cowell agreed: "There is this group of what I called 'super fans' and they were like promoters, these girls are crazy about One Direction. And I've got no idea why, I'm not a neuroscientist." Cut to ... Dr Stefan Koelsch, a neuroscientist. In one of the funniest scenes in

Spurlock's documentary, Koelsch explained that the reason One Direction appeals so much to their fans is all down to science. "As soon as Directioners listen to music and find the music pleasurable, what happens to the brain is that a neurochemical called dopamine is released and provides feelings of joy, and happiness. Shivers, goosebumps, strong pleasure. The girls are not crazy, the girls are just excited."

**Left:** Harry takes pole position during a performance at Z100's Jingle Ball 2012, Madison Square Garden, New York, December 7.

**Above:** Harry delights his fans outside the 28th Annual ARIA Awards 2014, Sydney, Australia, November 26.

**Overleaf:** Harry at the world premiere of *This Is Us* at the Empire, Leicester Square, London, August 20, 2013.

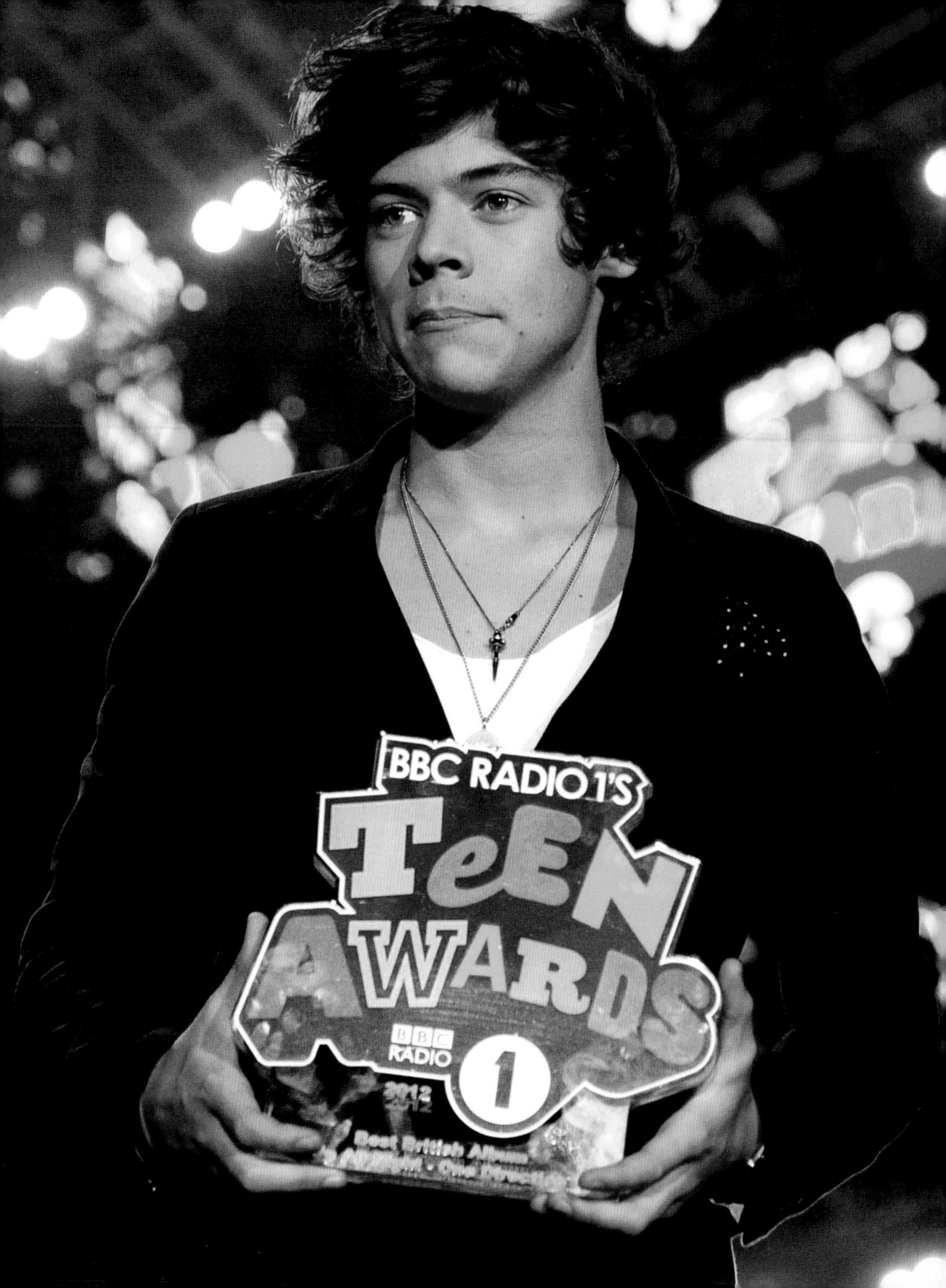
BBC RADIO 1'S
TEEN
AWARDS
BBC RADIO 1
2012

# "First thought was, could this work in America? There's not much of a track record of any British boy bands breaking in America."

ROB STRINGER, CHAIRMAN OF COLUMBIA RECORDS

Simon Cowell, who has obviously seen his fair share of wannabes and nevergonnabes, confirmed that neither One Direction nor the Directioners were faking it. The band may have been "made" on a TV show, but that's where the manufacturing process stopped. "I haven't seen a worldwide reaction like this to a group for a very long time," he remarked at the time of their rise. "If we'd been having a conversation two years ago, I wouldn't have said they were going to debut at number one in America. That would have been ridiculous." Even Louis Walsh, one of Harry's earliest denouncers, admits the band is special: "I've never seen a band cause so much hysteria so early in their career." The band themselves were shell-shocked by just how many fans they attained in such a short space of time. "It's something that really surprised us at the start," said Harry. "It still surprises us now how many people seem to like us."

The reason behind this Beatlemania-like hysteria was simple: the band were allowed to be themselves. From the off, both their management team and Simon Cowell nurtured their individual personalities and allowed them more freedom than any "manufactured" boy band that had gone before. Indeed, if the manipulative and exploitative management of boy bands such as Backstreet Boys, NSYNC and Take That set the standard of what it meant to be in a boy band in the twentieth century, then One Direction in the twenty-first century were the band that broke – no, smashed to smithereens – that mould. "The thing is, when you're playing a part," Harry said, "eventually

it goes wrong. Eventually someone's going to see that that's not who you are. So, it's best to be yourself from the get-go." One Direction were different from any other boy band, and this was ultimately down to the boys themselves.

"We could not follow the boy-band stereotypes, choreographed dance routine, then everything's the same," said Louis. Zayn agreed: "We didn't want to just follow the boy-band formula. We didn't want to do any dancing. We just wanted to be five dudes in a band."

**Left:** Harry holds the band's BBC Radio One Teen Award for Best British Album for *Up All Night*.

**Above:** Harry and Simon attend the *This Is Us* world premiere after party in London, August 20, 2013.

## "People who know me know what's true and what's not."

**Left:** Harry's multi-million dollar smile breaks as many hearts as it fixes.

**Right:** Man in the middle, Harry performs onstage during the 2012 MTV Video Music Awards, Los Angeles, California, September 6.

Thankfully, the band's choreographer was happy with this news. "I met the boys first when they came off *X Factor*. It was quite apparent to me, at the beginning, that there would be no jazz hands or spirit fingers." Harry also agreed: "Simon kind of hung back a bit and let us do what we wanted to do with it. I think that was good because it made things a bit more authentic. He still has the last say on everything we do. When we first met Simon, we'd go into the dressing room and talk to him normally. And then we came out, we'd be like, 'We've just been in the same room as Simon Cowell, had some bananas' ... it was so weird! We'll always be growing up. I'm just glad that we did it from the start how we want to do it."

Between 2012 and 2014, when the band really hit their stride, both as brothers in arms and musicians, there was a definite shift in the band's output and aesthetic. Like the Beatles before them, the band were growing up and growing older in front of their fans'

eyes, and it was all too plain to see. "The good thing about us," Niall said, "are the fans growing up with us. You know when people always say on interviews, 'Do you think the fans will grow up with you?' The truth is they've already grown up with us." This gave the band the freedom to develop. In 2013, Harry said: "I think the nice thing is that even though three years is not a long amount of time, we kind of feel like we now know what band we are. So, there are less things going into it like 'How do we want to do this? How do we want to that?' because it is who we are now."

During this time, the band's sound changed dramatically – from the power pop and slick beats of their earlier hits, such as 'What Makes You Beautiful' and 'Little Things', to the more mature, more musically minded tracks of 'You & I' and 'Drag Me Down'. "We've always described our sound as a bit more guitar-driven than normal pop music," Liam said of their music. "Kind of Pink in a boy-band form."

Harry agreed: "We like pop music but instead of using synths, we like using our hands. Guitars. Drums ..."

It was also throughout 2012–2013, as the band were entering into a new phase and growing into mature young men, that Morgan Spurlock recorded his documentary *This Is Us*. It captured the band not only behind the scenes, and at their most revealing, but also at the point when they were making that change into adulthood. Before cameras started rolling, the band were definitely still boys. With the premiere of the film in 2013, and their newfound black-clad leatherwear and super-cool fashion styles, it was clear that the band were now men, and were yearning to be taken seriously not only as musicians but as people too. No longer were the band given two packets of Haribo at 5 p.m. every day by their publicist, as was once claimed. Now the boys were attending fashion shows, *GQ* award shows, and, with the start of their next world tour, the aptly named Up All Night, they were also drinking.

"We don't really go out," Niall said, "but this tour will be different because we're all 18 now."

With the band often unable to get across their true emotions to their fans, Spurlock's *This Is Us* was designed to give their fans the AAA treatment, something sorely missing when they go on tour. Being "taken from the venue to the hotel and whatever else, you don't really see much in between" means that making a tangible connection with their fans is challenging.

Said Harry, "*This Is Us* is really a thank you to fans really, for sticking with us. We wanted to show them the real us, because social media and interviews don't really give you the chance to get to know someone." Harry's opinions on the limitations of social media platforms such as Twitter are clear: "You've only got, what, 140 characters? Fans want to get to know you and you can interact a bit, but we can't really put across who we are as people.

I really think *This Is Us* will help." It's something the whole band have spoken out about, with Niall famously saying, "It is really frustrating that you can't just stop and talk to them and tell them what they've done for us."

The documentary was announced by the band on *The Today Show* on November 12, 2012. It premiered on August 29, 2013 and was a worldwide box office success. Naturally. And yet the film itself had been a bit of a gamble for all concerned. The band was going through a change in direction, and Spurlock was a surprise choice for the global icons. His previous independent film may have been Oscar-nominated, but *Super Size Me* was about eating at McDonald's every day for a year. Now he was capturing intimate moments with the band, which certainly got fans' tongues wagging and raised more than a few eyebrows inside the One Direction inner circle. The band, however, were unconcerned.

"We really liked Morgan's style of filmmaking," Harry said. "Whatever Morgan does, he always seems to get right into it – he immerses himself into that world. And that's what we wanted; it's nerve-wracking letting people into our lives, even if cameras were following us around on *The X Factor* for 10 weeks. We needed someone we could trust because we were actually scared. But we've never said to him: 'Stop filming, this is private.' We really did want everything about us to go in. It wasn't a massive stress or anything, not something you thought about every day because the whole point of the film was to just have a normal day while the cameras were there rather than do a lot of stuff for the camera. When it was done, it was exciting to just see the next step. That was the fun bit."

This behind-the-scenes documentation of the group at their most intimate is one of the band's greatest achievements – it allows fans in at a time when so many other bands would have tried to keep them out. As it turned out, the director felt a genuine bond with what the band were going through, having experienced a similarly rapid ascent to fame himself. This allowed a natural chemistry between the group and the director to form, which meant he could dive deeper and get closer than perhaps any other director.

**Right:** One Direction pose in pastel colours for a photo shoot in Sweden, 2012.

This is at the centre of the film's ultimate success. Spurlock explained: "I do understand something of what it is like because after my breakthrough with *Super Size Me* everything went a bit nuts for me too. And then people were pretty quick to say, 'Oh who's this idiot – he's got no chance.' So, I understand what the boys go through when they're dismissed as little mannequins who dance and sing. But mainly, we built a rapport just through hanging out. They could see that I was investing in them, and they came to allow themselves to be vulnerable to me, I think."

More than half the film's scenes show the band having fun backstage – unthinkable for other groups of a similar stature – and with the film's release the second phase of One Direction's career had begun. But, after being followed around by cameras for the best part of six months, each member of the group was beginning to seek his own independence, and exhaustion and career fatigue began to show. "I always feel kind of out of breath," Harry said around this time. "We've just had a break. I was ill at home for the first five days." It was Liam who summed it up best. "I think of it like this: there are a lot of people who get paid a lot for doing not much at all – you know, like socialites who get paid for appearing in reality shows or people who earn like a million pounds a day working a couple of hours buying and selling shares – but what we earn we earn for doing an awful lot. We are constantly working." This constant work, being "bored to death in hotel rooms" and travelling from venue to hotel without seeing any of the culture that exists between the two, started to weigh heavily on the band. Niall was desperate to backpack around Australia and Vietnam like so many of his friends from home had done. He was sick of luxury hotels; he'd done them all. Louis became a father himself but was also coming to terms with his mother's diagnosis of terminal cancer, which would eventually take her away from him in 2016. Liam was being romantically linked to Cheryl Cole, and Zayn had effectively checked out of life in the band, causing tensions and stress that added to the band's overall discontentment.

During 1D's rise to fame, the release of their multi-million debut album *Up All Night* and the first world tour, Harry did not succumb to the pressures of Harrymania, a global phenomenon that made him the natural front man of the ensemble. There was just something about the singer, something that put him front and centre.

# "I'm 100 per cent in this band. I still want to be touring with One Direction in ten years. I'll be doing it until I'm old and people are telling me to stop."

**Left:** Harry's trademark curls and smile on display, Sweden, 2012.

**Overleaf:** Harry at the 28th Annual ARIA Awards 2014, Sydney, Australia November 26.

It might have been his curls, his handsome looks, his style, his cheeky attitude – or something else entirely – but it was Harry Styles who became the flashing beacon for the band on the world stage. Fame and fortune had arrived for Harry. And with it, came fans. Millions and millions of them. They were, and still are, affectionately referred to as Directioners. And as one, they were very, very loud.

Harry said: "There are a lot of things that come with the life you could get lost in. But you have to let it be what it is. I've learnt not to take everything too seriously." Staying focused and centred as the world started spinning out of control is why Harry is still here with us today, having not jeopardized his career with Bieberesque antics. During the height of Harrymania when every move of his was scrutinized not just by his fans but by those waiting for him to make a mistake, the singer himself noted: "I can see how you could get dragged into the bad stuff. But I've got good friends around me, good family. I think I've got my head screwed on." To this day, and despite the odds, Harry has yet to crash.. Fame, he observes, is a funny old thing. "I feel like when people label people as famous, they take away a lot of substance that they have as a person. So, you don't remember someone as 'He was funny', or 'They were really nice and giving'. It's like 'They were famous', and then it becomes a thing where anything after that, whatever you choose to do afterwards ... if it's not as famous, or more famous than it was before, it's considered a failure. And that's a shame, because it's not a failure, always."

As one-fifth of One Direction, Harry Styles became one of the most photographed human beings of the twenty-first century. The five were modern-day musical icons, made famous in a world of YouTube, TV singing competitions and social media, though it was actually their natural charisma and chemistry that appealed to millions of fans all over the world. It was to last five glorious years – a great run for any boy band.

Harry once said, "Here in One Direction we love to celebrate love, and love is love." And, should a fitting epitaph be required for the band – which is officially "on hiatus" though its members have gone their separate ways since 2015 – Then Harry's comment sums up the band's career perfectly.

**Right:** A rare moment of sitting still during their chaotic schedule, Harry and the gang make taking a break look good.

For One Direction, right from the start, were always five individuals, five separate but complementary personalities uniting as one, so it was always going to be a challenge to keep the band together for the long term. As it turns out, five years was the perfect amount of time for the band to align their personalities, become best friends, conquer the world, and walk away before things got nasty, as is so often the case with boy bands or bands who stay together too long – naming no names! "We're lucky that we do get on," Harry said at the beginning of the band's tenure as the Biggest Band in the World. "The relationship that I've grown with these four boys who I didn't know four years ago is absolutely insane and it's incredible."

Over the course of five years, 1D broke every musical record possible. And they didn't just break the records. They smashed them to smithereens, winning six Guinness World Records during their tenure as World's Biggest Band. Their debut album, Up All Night, was also a bestseller, becoming the UK's fastest-selling debut album of 2011. Their second album, Take Me Home, topped the charts in 34 countries. The accompanying tour travelled to 100 countries, including a six-date sell-out at London's O2 Arena – never before achieved.

Their third album, Midnight Memories, was the world's biggest-selling album in 2013. They sold more than 17 million records worldwide, across four albums. Their 2013 documentary, One Direction: This Is Us, was a genuine box office blockbuster. In 2014, Billboard announced that 1D were artist of the year. At the halfway point of 2015, the band released their final album, Made in the A.M., yet another global number one. At that time, they had more than four billion views on YouTube. They had outstripped the sales of every boy band ever and had a legion of devoted Directioners that made fans of other boy bands seem pale by comparison. "You get moments all the time that kind of make you pinch yourself, some of them make you quite emotional," Harry remembered. "Winning a BRIT was a big moment because we were just so excited to be at the awards in the first place. Selling out Madison Square Garden was pretty amazing too. Then we woke to the news that our UK tour was sold out. It was crazy."

By the end of the year 2015, the five boys were exhausted. But telling the world, and their fans, that they were over was a decision they had to consider carefully. The words "indefinite hiatus" were deployed to let their fans down gently. "You know, I think everyone needs a little bit of a break now, and a sit down and a stop, to kind of take in all the great things that've happened," Liam Payne explained. In a little over five years, each member of the band had gone from being paid £30 a day as *X Factor* auditioners to being worth more than £40 million each. As Harry's stepfather, Robin, once said: "Harry went to an audition and never came home again." Now the whole band realized they needed to go home. So they called it a day. To use Harry's now-famous phrase, they were "One and done".

**Left:** The boys pose in the press room during MTV's Video Music Awards 2012, Los Angeles, California, September 6.

**Below:** As the boys began to grow up, so did their fashion styles.

**Overleaf:** One Direction perform at HMV Hammersmith Apollo, London, January 22, 2012.

# Chapter Four
## ONE AND DONE

# ONE AND DONE

AT THE END OF 2015, WORD TRAVELLED
AROUND THE WORLD THAT 1D WERE
ABOUT TO ENTER AN "EXTENDED
HIATUS". FANS WERE, AND STILL ARE,
DEVASTATED; 1D WERE SEEMINGLY NO
MORE. BUT, OF COURSE, FOR HARRY
STYLES, THE END OF 1D WAS JUST THE
VERY BEGINNING ...

But let's take this chapter slowly. This is one of the
most traumatic periods of young Harry's career. A time
defined by difficult decisions. A time when Harry had
to answer the question: "What do I do if I'm not in 1D?"

In July 2016, 1D disappeared from the world on an
"extended hiatus for 18 months" with the promise
from all remaining members that one day the band
would resurface and come to reclaim their crown as
the World's Biggest Band. Almost two years later,
with each member enjoying solo success, the time
when 1D might return has most likely come and gone.
It seems the good ship 1D will never sail again.

"Please don't forget us, we will always be here for
you, you guys are the most incredible fans." So said
Harry as 1D walked off-stage of their final show on
*The X Factor* in December 2015. This group of singing
misfits had come full circle since that iconic moment
when they blossomed to life on the same stage in 2010.

**Right:** Then there were four: The band play their final live show,
Sheffield Arena, October 31, 2015.

The band was going out on top, as friends. Besides, it's not like they could go any higher – they had achieved everything that is possible, and much more too.

"It's really hard to go from doing a show with thousands of people there to your hotel room – from being around people to nothing," said Harry, immediately after 1D took a bow for perhaps the final time. "After five years of doing that, I learnt a lot about myself. There's no textbook telling you how to go through that stuff."

Towards the end of 1D, life on the road had become tiring. As Harry put it: "Life in 1D had become like a Wes Anderson movie. Cut. Cut. New location. Quick cut. New location. Cut. Cut. Show. Shower. Hard cut. Sleep." The monotony of touring had become hard work and the group were at risk of burning out both as individuals and as friends.

The demise of 1D started, as everyone knows, with the departure of Zayn Malik in March 2015. Looking back now, it's plain to see that Zayn's time in 1D caused the singer much anxiety: Stage fright, eating disorders, feeling uncomfortable in his own skin, performing other people's songs, feeling out of place. For Zayn, 1D was a cursed blessing.

"After five incredible years Zayn Malik has decided to leave One Direction," began the official announcement of Zayn's departure. "Niall, Harry, Liam and Louis will continue as a four-piece and look forward to the forthcoming concerts of their world tour and recording their fifth album, due to be released later this year." Zayn then posted his own words directly underneath: "My life with One Direction has been more than I could ever have imagined. But, after five years, I feel like it is now the right time for me to leave the band. I'd like to apologise to the fans if I've let anyone down, but I have to do what feels right in my heart. I am leaving because I want to be a normal 22-year-old who is able to relax and have some private time out of the spotlight. I know I have four friends for life in Louis, Liam, Harry and Niall. I know they will continue to be the best band in the world."

This statement would remain the only word from Zayn for more than a year. At the time, and up until the band's final TV performance in December 2015, the remaining four members remained tight-lipped about their exiting fifth member. Indeed, their only comment was attached to the Facebook page. "We're really sad to see Zayn go, but we totally respect his decision and send him all our love for the future. The past five years have been beyond amazing, we've gone through so much together, so we will always be friends. The four of us will now continue. We're looking forward to recording the new album and seeing all the fans on the next stage of the world tour."

There were those who read between the lines. It was clear that some of the words spoken between the five guys were being kept hush-hush, made evident by the fact that Simon Cowell had the final word on the official announcement: "I would like to say thank you to Zayn for everything he has done for One Direction. Since I first met Zayn in 2010, I have grown very, very fond – and immensely proud – of him. I have seen him grow in confidence and I am truly sorry to see him leave. As for One Direction, fans can rest assured that Niall, Liam, Harry and Louis are hugely excited about the future of the band."

It wasn't until January 2016, and the release of Zayn's debut single 'Pillowtalk', that the singer opened up much more about the real reasons he decided to quite the group. "There was never any room for me to experiment creatively. If I would sing a hook or a verse slightly R&B, or slightly myself, it would always be recorded 50 times until there was a straight version that was pop, generic as fuck, so they could use that version. Whenever I would suggest something, it was like it didn't fit us … I wasn't 100 per cent behind the music. It wasn't me." Interviewed by Zane Lowe for Beats 1 Radio, Malik didn't hold back: "I think I always wanted to go, from the first year. I never really wanted to be there, like, in the band. I just gave it a go because it was there at the time and then when I realized the direction we were going in – mind the pun – with the music, I instantly realized it wasn't for me. I realized I couldn't put any input in, I couldn't give my opinion on this or not because it didn't fit the grain of what we were as a band and what we represented. That's when it became frustrating for me. When I was leaving the band, they didn't want me to leave, but they couldn't talk me out of it at that point. I had already made my mind up."

**Left:** Harry performs to the fans at 99.7's NOW! Triple Ho Show, San Jose, California, December 2, 2015.

**Below:** 1D attend the BBC Music Awards in style, Genting Arena, Birmingham, December 10, 2015.

The fans were dismayed by Zayn's comments. His former bandmates, too, were left reeling at the betrayal. It was Harry who came out first with a reply: "I think it's a shame he felt that way, but I never wish anything but luck to anyone doing what they love. If you're not enjoying something and need to do something else, you absolutely should do that. I'm glad he's doing what he likes, and good luck to him. I mean, yes, obviously. If anyone is ever going through anything, you always feel like you should know, so you could have done something. But it's not always how it goes, is it? In the same way that I don't talk about stuff, other people don't always talk about stuff, and maybe that's how they deal with stuff."

Harry had been singled out by Zayn, who made a stinging comment about the relationship: "To be honest, I never really spoke to Harry even when I was in the band ... So I didn't really expect that much of a relationship with him." Throughout the final year or so of the band's touring schedule and past the release of *Midnight Memories*, many reports about Harry and Zayn's "falling out" had been published, though nothing substantiated, the stories being killed off – no doubt, by the band's management, eager to keep things on a civil footing for the sake of the fans already distraught by Zayn's departure. As with the split of Take That in the 1990s, when a Samaritans Helpline was set up to help fans deal with the break-up, 1D's management were concerned for the fans' wellbeing.

The four remaining members of the band initially kept quiet about Zayn's departure, other than their

**Above:** If looks could kill: Harry smoulders at the BBC Music Awards Birmingham, 2015.

**Right:** Harry poses for the cameras on the red carpet at the British Fashion Awards 2014, London, December 1.

Facebook post, until they appeared on *The Late, Late Show with James Corden*. Liam said: "At first, we were a little bit angry, we were surprised. I think we all knew the general vibe that Zayn was feeling. You could sort of tell. There's certain parts of this job Zayn loved and there's certain parts … we were angry at first and then it was just more disappointed. We wish him the best of luck with whatever he gets up to. There's no hard feelings. It's been a tough few weeks, probably the toughest since the band was formed five years ago. We're gutted that Zayn chose to leave, but now after a few performances as

a four-piece, we're feeling confident and are determined to carry on stronger than ever."

With Zayn gone – despite tabloid reports of him claiming – "I tried to reach out and be their friend, but they haven't even replied to any of my calls or texts" – the four boys knew they had to work even harder to stay strong for each other. "One thing that was good is that it made us really bond," says Harry. "It made us look at what we had and really know we wanted to keep it. It also made us really focus on making the best album we could.

You go through so much together as a band that no one really understands, but ultimately it just makes you closer."

Inevitably, of course, 1D could not continue as a united four-piece following Zayn's departure. Liam initially tried to be upbeat, saying of the situation: "I like that quote about teabags and hot water. You can only test how strong you are when you get put in hot water. We've been tested, but it's actually made us stronger. We've actually taken a lot of strength from our fans who have never given up on us, never believed it was over. It's not over. And yes, we're taking a break, but we need one. We have done four tours, five albums, but we will be coming back. We don't want this to end."

The remaining four members had to dig deep, come out fighting and find themselves again. After all, they had a tour to perform and a new number one album, *Made in the A.M.*, to promote. But, the end was nigh. Everyone could feel it.

For the first couple of world tours, the band had been so excited to be together conquering the world that they never realized how emotionally exhausting it was. They would enjoy a drink or two and attend parties as often as possible. "But for me," Harry stated in a 2017 interview, "the albums got higher, so they become harder to sing, so I knew if I didn't come off stage and go to bed I wouldn't be able to sing the next night. Also, it's just not for me. I'd rather wake up with a clear head."

For Harry, January 2016 was all about waking up with a clear head and a New Year resolution after the break-up of One Direction.

**Above:** On the road again, Miller Park Stadium, Milwaukee, August 25, 2015.

**Right:** Harry proudly holds One Direction's Artist of the Year Award at the 2015 American Music Awards, November 22.

**Overleaf:** The final show, Sheffield Arena, October 31, 2015.

"In our free time we sit around and I play guitar and we jam like that, but the album that we're making at the moment is a bit edgier."

"

I didn't want to exhaust our
fan base. If you're short-
sighted, you can think, 'Let's
just keep touring', but we
all thought too much of the
group than to let that happen.
You realize you're exhausted
and you don't want to drain
people's belief in you.

"

During the final album and Where We Are Now world tour, rumours had begun to circulate about Harry signing a record deal, and entering a recording studio with Ryan Tedder, songwriter to the stars.

Then, in July 2016, it was announced that Harry had signed a record-breaking deal – £80 million for five albums with Columbia Records. A record executive for Harry's new label claimed: "Harry has always been One Direction's most popular member and it's obvious that we want to secure him. He's a global superstar. Zayn will get to release an album first, as he left the band earlier, but the most excitement is about what Harry is going to do. Everyone wants to know what his solo material will sound like, there's also a lot of pressure to get it right. Harry is a smart guy and is really good at surrounding himself with talented people."

The talk now was that this was the end of the band for good. Was Harry's record deal, followed by the announcement of Liam's solo record deal a mere two weeks later, the final nail in the coffin? Each member has categorically denied that this is the end of 1D, though Louis has said of this time, "It wasn't necessarily a nice conversation. I could see where it was going." Harry, Liam and Niall may have solo deals,

while Louis has taken time off to be a father, work a bit in TV and deal with the death of his mother, but talks of a reunion have come thick and fast from all camps. No one has come out and clarified the matter, and even Simon Cowell was left in the dark. In an interview with *Billboard*, he said: "I don't know if it's a hiatus or a breakup, to be honest. In a weird way, I don't want to know. I don't think they've had enough time to experience what it's like not being in the group to really answer that. Whenever I was with them, we talked about it, and I couldn't argue with them. They had achieved so much in a short period of time, and I didn't want them to get jaded. As I've gotten older, I've learned to trust people more, particularly artists. They'll decide when they want to come back together."

Should the band ever reunite, it will certainly be the hottest ticket in town. But with each member going their own separate ways and appearing to be busier by the year, it seems extremely unlikely, despite the seemingly ever-present press frenzy.

**Above:** Harry rocks Dick Clark's New Year's Rockin' Eve, hosted by Ryan Seacrest, December 31, 2016.

# "The nice thing for me is that I'm not coming away from the band feeling like I wasn't able to do what I wanted to do. I loved it and it was what I wanted but I'm enjoying writing at the moment; trying new things."

"Never say never" is the optimistic phrase they all use. Harry has said: "When we started people always asked, where do you think you'll be in five years? It's a difficult question to answer. I would never say we'll never do anything again but it's good for us to be exploring different things. Maybe at some point everyone will want to do something again but it'll be better if it happens naturally like, 'Hey, we all really want to do this again.' If that were to happen it would be amazing. I would never rule that out. It's the most important, greatest thing that ever happened to me, being in that band. It completely changed my life. But, I feel pretty lucky right now. I feel good about everything that happened with the band, I have no complaints or regrets."

It isn't just Harry who is cautiously keen on a reunion. The other members have all gone on record stating that a reunion in the future would never be ruled out. "I told my managers from the start: When One Direction comes knocking, fook what I'm doing. I don't give a shit if I sold out arenas or won Grammys. I wouldn't be doing this if it wasn't for that," Niall said hilariously, though he added: "When it will be, I don't know. I prefer not to do it after I'm 40. I'd prefer the next few years."

Louis too was just as adamant there would be

a return: "There is no question of if – it's a must. And I think we're all on the same page with that one. It would be too difficult for any of us to say no. It is so frustrating when I read stories in the press saying we don't like each other. I feel like a big brother to all of the boys. When I see videos of Niall playing to a stadium or Harry standing next to people like Tom Hardy at a film premiere, I just feel so proud. It's amazing."

As for Zayn, he has gone on record saying: "Who knows? I don't know. If the time was right and that was the thing to do, then I would make that decision when it came around." That's not a no, which is what will keep the fans satisfied for now. And although the question of whether we will ever see these five famous friends in the same room together is one that no one can answer, everyone is, according to Harry, still friends: "Everyone's working so much at the moment, but I've seen them and we've hung out."

1D may have fractured, but Harry Styles has carved out an entirely new career for himself. Yes, 2016 was the year that saw him reinvent himself. First, it was time for some well-deserved time off.

**Left:** Harry shows off his star power at the 2015 American Music Awards, November 22.

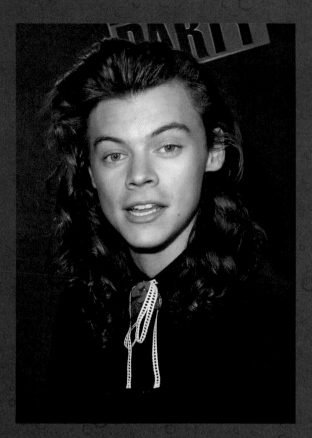

"I've always wondered how Harry's brain works. He's kind of like a weird comedian." NIALL HORAN

# "I love the band, and would never rule out anything in the future. The band changed my life, gave me everything."

But, as we've come to know Harry isn't happy unless he's keeping busy. And for Harry that could mean turning up at fashion shows or popping in to see Nick Grimshaw on his BBC Radio show.

"I like to keep busy and I like to see my mates," Harry has said of his time off. "I keep wondering whether I should actually watch those great shows that everyone else talks about and I've missed, like *Mad Men* and *Breaking Bad*. Or should I just move on?" Moving on is what he did. But not in the way anyone expected. While his former bandmates were content with concentrating on their solo records and gearing up for their own headline tours, Harry, being Harry, decided to do something different. "I started my album the end of February in 2016 for three weeks and had to stop for five months when I went to do a movie. I came back to it in July and finished writing it in December," he said. But, this wasn't just any rom-com chick flick or indie hipster film; this was Christopher Nolan's epic Second World War blockbuster *Dunkirk*. The world was about to see Harry Styles in a whole new light …

**Opposite, Left:** Harry and the boys rock up at Dick Clark's New Year's Rockin 'Eve with Ryan Seacrest 2016, December 31, 2015.

**Opposite, Right:** Proudly presenting his first film, *Dunkirk*, Harry the actor had arrived, July 16, 2017.

**Right:** Harry arrives at BBC Radio 2 Studios, London, to promote his album on Nick Grimshaw's show, May 12, 2017.

# Chapter Five
## THE TRANSFORMATION OF HARRY STYLES

# THE TRANSFORMATION OF HARRY STYLES

HARRY STYLES COULD NOT BE NAMED MORE PERFECTLY. ALWAYS THE MOST STYLISH MEMBER IN ONE DIRECTION, HARRY HAS BEEN PUTTING ON AND PULLING OFF SOME RATHER EXCELLENT, AND ECCENTRIC, FASHIONS OVER THE PAST FEW YEARS, FOR WHICH HE HAS BECOME (IN)FAMOUS. HIS 2017 HEADLINE SOLO TOUR SAW HIM WEAR A NEW, AND DIFFERENT, SELECTION OF SUITS EVERY SINGLE NIGHT.

It was in 2013, when Harry turned 19, that One Direction's wild child started to break free from the boy-band mould. He ditched his Jack Wills T-shirts and khaki trousers, threw out his hoodies and tracksuits, and pledged a new allegiance to Gucci, Burberry and Saint Laurent. The singer became increasingly more tattooed (inspiration he took from his idol David Beckham and close friend Ed Sheeran), and he now has more than 50 of them. With his scraggy long hair causing a stir everywhere it went, it was clear that Harry wanted to be seen as more of an individual, and to stand out from his colleagues – perhaps even becoming something of a fashion icon. With a huge array of natty printed satin shirts, leather boots, silk scarves, tuxedo jackets, candyfloss pink suits, Harry was always suited and booted (often in high heels) and dressed to impress at every premiere, after-show or fashion show.

**This Page:** Harry the *X Factor* finalist arrives at a dance studio, London, October 13, 2010.

**Right:** Hollywood Harry appears at SiriusXM, Roxy Theatre, California, May 17, 2017.

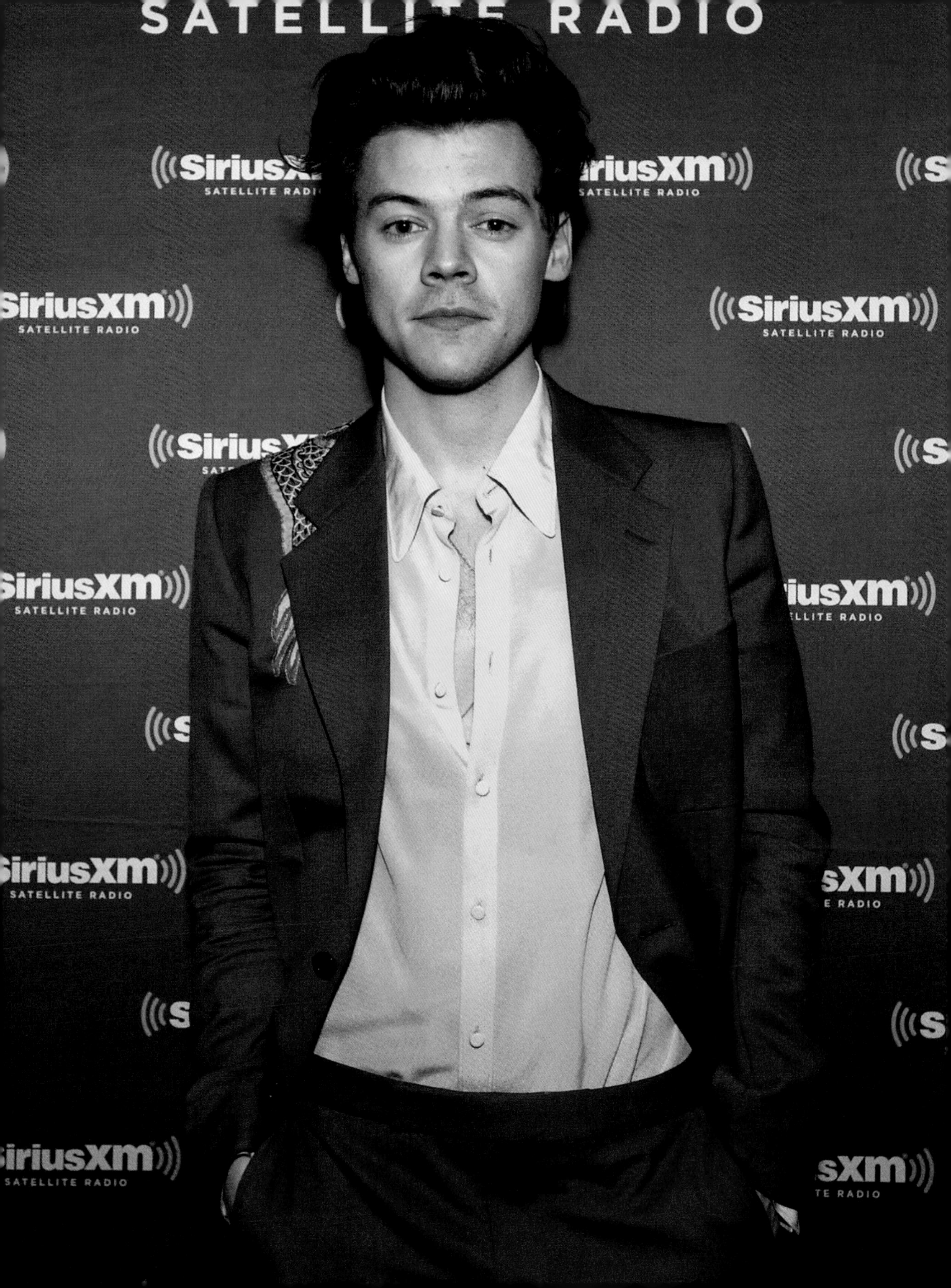
SATELLITE RADIO
SiriusXM
SATELLITE RADIO

"I love an accessory as much as the next person."

"**I want to shave my hair off, and no one will really let me. Everyone's telling me not to do it. And my argument is, like, I think my popularity is in my face, and not my hair.**"

Harry's sartorial flare rubbed off on his band mates, but it was Harry who was always ahead of the pack, refusing to bend to a particular image. His fans loved him for his independence, his individuality and his ability to pull off anything he put on; his clothes became a metaphor for his personality. By 2014, when the band took to the road once more for their Where We Are world tour, it was increasingly rare to see Harry not draped in his finest. He knew people would stare at him, so he figured he might as well make it worth their while and give them something awesome to stare at!

To make Harry's foray into fashion official, he was voted – by the public, no less – the winner of the British Style Awards 2013. By doing so he beat David Beckham, Kate Moss, the Duchess of Cambridge and Cara Delevingne to the crown. The award "recognises an individual who most embodies the spirit of London and is an international ambassador for London as a leading creative fashion capital". We think that sums up Harry perfectly. Accepting his award, he kept his speech short and sweet: "This is very, very kind."

**Left:** Harry the hipster goes casual at Capital FM's Summertime Ball, Wembley Stadium, London, June 6, 2015.

**Above:** Spotted on the street in Los Angeles, California, January 20, 2016.

# Chapter Six

## A NEW DIRECTION

# A NEW DIRECTION

SINGER. ACTOR. FASHION ICON. HARRY STYLES MAKES ALL OF THESE THINGS
LOOK SO EASY. NOW ANOTHER STRING HAS BEEN ADDED TO HARRY'S BOW
– SONGWRITER. SINCE THE BEGINNING OF ONE DIRECTION, HARRY WAS ALWAYS
VOCAL ABOUT PARTICIPATING IN THE WRITING OF THEIR BIGGEST HITS, EVEN IF HE
LACKED THE EXPERIENCE AND CONFIDENCE. AND WITH THE RELEASE OF HIS DEBUT
ALBUM IN 2017, IT IS NOW CLEAR THAT HARRY IS A SONGWRITING FORCE TO BE
RECKONED WITH. NOR WAS IT JUST MUSIC THAT CAPTURED HARRY'S ATTENTION;
ACTING HAS PLAYED A PROMINENT ROLE IN HELPING THE YOUNG SINGER BLOSSOM
FROM HIS 1D CHRYSALIS INTO SOMETHING GREATER THAN EVEN HIS HARSHEST
CRITICS COULD HAVE COMPREHENDED. HARRY STYLES IS NOW A BUSINESSMAN,
A BRAND, A SUCCESSFUL SOLO ARTIST, AND THE MOST FAMOUS HARRY IN THE
WORLD (SORRY, POTTER FANS).

In 2017, at the relatively young age of 23, Harry Styles' career spun off into a new orbit among the stars. He was just 16 when he entered the pop universe, auditioning for *The X Factor* in 2010. Today, he has more than 15 million Facebook fans, more than 22 million followers on Instagram and 31 million Twitter devotees, who await every single one of his allotted 140 characters. In their five and a half years of existence, One Direction sold more than 20 million albums. But he knew that all these achievements would forever be compared to the reaction by his fans of his debut self-titled debut album, released in May 2017. Thankfully, it achieved the highest first week sales in the United States by any British male solo artist ever – and further cemented Styles' place in the pantheon of pop greats.

Now out on his own, and for the first time in his professional career, Harry got to call the shots on all aspects of his music – from choosing what to wear on stage and designing the album cover to attending promotion and business meetings. While he has a team of "incredible people" around him helping him making smart decisions, Harry ultimately was in charge. No longer protected by management or other band members, he was making the choices that would affect and impact his future. For Harry it was nerve-wracking, but it was time to grow up and show the world what he could do. "I've never done it before, been across absolutely everything, but it's been good. Every decision I've made since I was 16 was made in a democracy.

**Left:** Attending the preview screening of *Dunkirk* at BFI Southbank, Harry looks all grown up, July 13, 2017.

I felt like it was time to make a decision about the future … and maybe I shouldn't rely on others. I wanted to step up." From his clothing to the colour scheme of his album design, Harry's fingerprints are everywhere. "They send one font," Harry said of choosing his debut album's cover typography, an important aesthetic design decision for his brand, "and you're like 'Well, that's not the right font!' And you didn't think you were bothered about fonts. That's when you feel like you're adminning … and then you realize how particular you are about fonts."

On May 12, 2017, Harry Styles went from boy band heartthrob to bona fide breakthrough male artist. After 12 months in the making, the singer released his ten-song debut album. To prove that he had finally arrived as an artist in his own right, he kept the album's title short, sweet and to the point. He called it *Harry Styles*. That was not just an album title – it was a declaration that the real Harry Styles had arrived. "This album has made me realize the Harry in 1D was kind of the digitized Harry, almost like a character," he said. "I don't think people know a lot of the sides of him that are on this album. You put it on and people are like, 'This is Harry Styles?'"

It goes without saying that the record went straight to number one and was a critical hit among Harry's loyal fan base, who had grown up alongside the singer and were ready to appreciate a more stripped back style and "natural" sound. Gone are the pulsing pop beats and sweet saccharine lyrics that defined 1D, replaced now by intricate acoustic guitars, twisted lovelorn lyrics and serious songwriting, which screams out Harry's singular personality. With more mature songs and loads of nods to the artists who defined the golden age of rock and pop in the 1960s and '70s, *Harry Styles* is the sound of now; the sound of who he wants to be and who he is – and not what other people expect him to be.

**Right:** Harry meets Harry: *Dunkirk* World Premiere, Odeon Leicester Square, London, July 13, 2017.

**Overleaf:** Stealing the spotlight at his debut album's iHeartRadio album-release party in New York, May 8, 2017.

As he told *Rolling Stone* in April 2017: "I didn't want to put out my first album and critics be like, 'He's tried to recreate the Sixties, Seventies, Eighties, Nineties.' Loads of amazing music was written then, but I'm not saying I wish I lived back then. I wanted to do something that sounds like me. I just keep pushing forward."

The album was recorded during the bookends of 2016, in between Harry's audition and critically acclaimed performance as Alex in Christopher Nolan's film, *Dunkirk*. Indeed, Harry claimed that it was the acting bug that helped him find his solo musical feet. "For a while before, all I thought about was stressing about what the album was going to be. The movie gave me a chance to completely step away from it for a bit and have a real break," he said. This break, or distraction, from writing music, and this dedication to another art form infused Harry with new influences and lyrical inspiration, which ultimately flavoured the album, giving it a unique and natural personality. For the six months that Harry and the character Alex were one and the same, exhausted on the beaches of the western French coast, Harry grew in confidence, and realized that in order to truly capture his sound and voice on record, he would need to get away from everything he knew. "I didn't want to just pick a sound and write ten of the same things," he said. So, with his famous, trademarked long curls shorn from his head, and his performance as Alex in the can, Harry took his new band to Jamaica. It was there that *Harry Styles* was born.

**Above:** Harry reflects during a photo-call for *Dunkirk*, ahead of the release of the movie, July 16, 2017.

Teenage-girl fans – they don't lie. If they like you, they're there. They don't act 'too cool'. They like you, and they tell you.

Arriving in Jamaica almost immediately after the *Dunkirk* experience, Harry and his band had a masterplan to capture Harry as the front man he himself desired. Alex Salibian (guitars, keyboards and production), Mitch Rowland (guitars and production), Clare Uchima (keyboards), Sarah Jones (drums) and Adam Prendergast (bass), along with Jeff Bhasker, Tyler Johnson, Ryan Nasci and other producers, would go on a journey together. Travelling inside Harry's mind and seeing what they found.

"I wanted to put out a piece of me that I haven't put out before," Harry said when promoting the album. "I didn't want to write stories. I wanted to write *my* stories, things that happened to me. The number one thing was, I wanted to be honest. I hadn't done that before."

After five years of singing songs predominately written by other songwriters, Harry had a vision for his first solo effort, right from the start. For the first time in his professional music career, Harry was able to use his voice to express his true self: "I don't think people want to hear me sing about going to bars, and how great everything is.

**Right:** "Pink is the true colour of rock and roll": Harry's candyfloss pink suit went down a treat with fans on the *Today Show* in New York.

## TRACKLISTING
*What's your favourite track?*

'Meet Me In The Hallway'
'Sign of the Times'
'Carolina'
'Two Ghosts'
'Sweet Creature'
'Only Angel'
'Kiwi'
'Ever Since New York'
'Woman'
'From The Dining Table'

The champagne popping ... who wants to hear about it? I don't want to hear my favourite artists talk about all the amazing shit they get to do. I want to hear, 'How did you feel when you were alone in that hotel room, because you chose to be alone?' With this album, rather than just go in and tell the story about what happened, I got to think about how it actually made me feel at the time."

The album, which Harry wrote in collaboration with producers and songwriters Jeff Bhasker, Tyler Johnson, Ryan Nasci, Mitch Rowland and Alex Salibian, was 70 songs long at one point! "We recorded 50 songs and ideas in Jamaica – and that's including, like, little ideas. I say there are 30 songs, probably." Once Harry began to have the time to

explore his songwriting abilities, all of a sudden lots of great ideas started to flow from him. And once that happened, songwriting became cathartic: "I found it really therapeutic to write. Sitting at an instrument, you allow yourself to be vulnerable in a different way to speaking to anyone, even if you know them really well. I found it to be therapy – things that I'd either not thought about for a long time or hadn't processed really because things had been moving so fast. We didn't get the six months to see what kind of shit you can work with. It was tough to really delve in and find out who you are as a writer when you're just kind of dipping your toe each time. To have time to live with a song, see what you love as a fan, chip at it, hone it and go for that ... it's heaven."

Turning 70 ideas into 10 viable songs that work well with each other is a tough assignment for any band. But for Harry, cutting through all the noise from the adventures he has already lived to get to the real person underneath was a challenge.

**Above:** Harry's first headline tour opens in style at The Masonic, San Francisco, California. September 19, 2017.

"I'll tell you this much, the first time I saw him pull out the guitar, I was, like, 'Oh damn, he can play!' He has a nice stroke. He has a feel and a sound and an emotion. He's a real musician." JEFF BHASKER

"I didn't know what my own voice was; I didn't know what might happen," Styles said. "So, it was really important to me that the only voice really was mine. I felt like if I stayed around places where I knew I was going to have people tell me what they think it should be ... I knew I was just going to get distracted and frustrated." The answer, as it turned out, was to escape to a place Harry had never been before, and where no one knew him. "I went to Jamaica because I didn't want to be around distractions. The thing with being in London, or LA, or pretty much anywhere that you know people, is it's tough, because you go into the studio for ten hours, and then, at some point, everyone has to eat, and you go home. I just wanted to really dive into it and immerse myself. It became this fluid thing that we were just doing all of the time, rather than going in from nine to five. I also didn't want to be around people who might tell me what [the music] should sound like."

Jeff Bhasker, one of the album's chief architects in relation to production and writing, agreed: "It was a 24/7 music fest: wake up, do some exercise, go to the studio all day, come home, eat dinner, write songs back at the house, go try out some ideas, maybe get excited and go back to the studio at 2 a.m. It was just a nonstop flow of creative ideas, which was great. It's never a bad thing to focus, isolate, and go a little island crazy."

One of Harry's other close collaborators on the project, songwriter Tom Hull (otherwise known as Kid Harpoon), supported Harry's immersion therapy.

"The thing that's incredible about Harry that I don't think people realize as much yet is that he drives it all. It's very much his taste. He's very musical; he plays guitar, plays piano and writes songs. He loves music. That was the hard thing, I think, in One Direction before. You've got a bunch of lads who all have different tastes in music and have their own personalities. Obviously, it's clear they've all done something different as solo artists."

Indeed, with Harry now unencumbered by the routines of being in the biggest band in the world, he is free to indulge his time and desires in whatever he fancies. As it turns out, he spends most of his time shopping for "really geeky" music equipment and texting his band about all the new music he has discovered. "He's turning me on to music I've never even heard of from, like, 1978," Hull said, "and he's texting people in the band 'Have you heard this? Have you heard that?' For someone where he's at, he just absolutely adores it, and it's inspiring for everyone underneath."

For this album, it was Harry Nilsson who laid the earworms in the other Harry's mind. "I listened to a lot of Harry Nilsson while making the album. His lyrics are honest, and so good, and I think it's because he's never trying to sound clever." "Honesty" is a word that kept swirling around Harry's mind, and it would be the only well from which he would drink inspiration. If a lyric, or song, wasn't honest, it didn't make the cut. This required Harry to be honest with himself and for others in the studio control room to be honest with Harry.

Jeff Bhasker explained the process: "This is 100 percent Harry. It's very much Harry's album and the music he wanted to make. And he was very specific what kind of ideas turn him on. He's pretty clear, in the coolest way, about what he likes and doesn't like, so it really got the album off on the right foot and finished on the right foot. In the first week, they did, like, 10 songs, half of which ended up on the album. As people absorb what this is and who he is, they'll see that he's his own thing. Obviously, we're trying to push the envelope of being a boy band, so early on, I was, like, 'the album has to be super edgy,' but then it was about knowing when to pull back up against the edge and be real. Which is ultimately what I think we landed on. I think I did push him in a lot of ways, but then I wanted him to have complete ownership of it and to sing what is really in his heart."

Being this real, and singing from the heart, is what makes the record such a rewarding listen – it is the sound of an emerging artist finding his feet. It's the not sound of a famous boy band member retreading old ground or making music by numbers. "Making this album is one of the best times I've ever had," said Harry. "But it's a much more vulnerable feeling coming to put it out than I've experienced before. Starting out with no reference points for the actual sound, the only thing that I knew I wanted to be was honest."

**Left:** Harry's natty suit draws cheers from the crowd at The Masonic, San Francisco, California, September 19, 2017.

**Above:** A momentous evening! Harry performs at LA's prestigious Hollywood Bowl for CBS RADIO's We Can Survive 2017 charity show, October 21, 2017.

"I didn't want to sit and edit lyrics. In the times of going, 'Oh, can I say that?' I wanted to be like, 'Yeah, I can – because that's what I wrote.'"

For two months, Harry and the band worked on the tracks, working out his own sound as well as a coherent track listing. It was with the writing of song 'Sign of the Times' that something clicked. His honest voice had arrived. He could hear his sound in his head: "I think I've always written bits of songs alone, and then I usually take stuff in and try to finish it with someone. 'Sign of the Times' was one of those where I just kind of wrote it. We basically ended up in a place where the album had a bunch of rock songs and a bunch of acoustic, kind of picked ballad songs. And I wrote 'Sign of the Times' and just felt like there was all this middle ground that I wanted to then explore. And I think that's the one that kind of started bridging us to different places in terms of experimenting a little more."

Everyone at the Gee Jam Hotel Recording Studio, Port Antonio, Jamaica, believed that 'Sign of the Times' was the starting gun that flavoured the sound and personality for the rest of the album. "That was kind of out there. And by the way, the song was made in four hours, from writing it to tracking it. That's part of the reason why it's so long because Harry just freestyled it towards the end. We tracked it like that and it was kind of awesome. Once we had it, we knew it was a winner. It starts out with Harry's voice sounding so great and then you hit them with the next verse and you've got 'em. It is a hit in that sense, but it was so long that we weren't sure if it could be the single. Thank God, Rob Stringer, head of Columbia Records said, 'I think you go with "Sign of the Times."' Then, we tried to do major surgery on it to try and make a radio edit and presented it to him and, he was, like, 'That's cool, but I think we should push the full-length.' We were looking at each other, like, what planet are we on that the head of the label says, 'Yeah, let's release a six-minute single!'"

**Left:** Fans go wild at Radio City Music Hall, New York, September 28, 2017.

**Overleaf:** A smaller venue than he's used to, Harry delights the audience at Radio City Music Hall, New York, September 28, 2017.

**"**I really wanted to make an album that I wanted to listen to. That was the only way I knew I wouldn't look back on it and regret it. It was more, 'What do I want to sit and listen to?' rather than, 'How do I shake up compared to what's on radio right now?**"**

**Right:** A new suit every night: the singer performing onstage at the 2017 iHeartRadio Music Festival, T-Mobile Arena, Las Vegas, Nevada, September 22.

It's no surprise that Harry's lead single from the album, his first ever single as a solo artist, was a song that not only echoed Harry's desire to be honest with himself but also highlighted his discontentment with the state of the world. The song is a combination of Harry looking inward and outward at the same time: "we gotta get away from here" expresses his disillusion, but the song also reveals his insistence that life can be better if we talk together and "open up". Harry said of the song: "We're in a difficult time, and I think we've been in many difficult times before. But we happen to be in a time where things happening around the world are absolutely impossible to ignore. I think it would've been strange to not acknowledge what was going on at all. For example, 'Sign of the Times', for me, it's looking at several different things. That's me commenting on different things. Everything you were talking about – just the state of the world at the moment. It's very much me looking at that. It's a time when it's very easy to feel incredibly sad about a lot of things. It's also nice sometimes to remember that while there's a lot of bad stuff, there's also a lot of amazing people doing amazing things in the world. I think it would have been weird for me to write an album and not acknowledge that there's anything bad going on in the world. And I think we were writing it from a place of – you have five minutes to say, 'It's going to be all right.'"

Thankfully, Harry's song got the nod of approval from his former mentor Simon Cowell. "Simon called after hearing an advance copy of 'Sign of the Times'. He said he really liked it and he was very proud of me. It was very friendly ... not like past phone calls haven't been friendly, but I didn't get that nervy 'the boss is calling' feel, which was nice."

With 'Sign of the Times' in the bag, Harry's confidence grew and other songs tumbled out of his excited mind. One of them, the final song on the album, grew to become Harry's first solo masterpiece. And, naturally, it's a song that comes straight from the depths of Harry's soul. "My favourite from the album is 'From The Dining Table'. It's just personal, and I don't feel like I've written a song like this before." The track's lyrical edgy qualities demand that your ears stand up and listen. We're not in boy band territory anymore: *Woke up alone in this hotel room, played with myself where were you/ Fell back asleep, got drunk by noon, I've never felt less cool.*

"I'd say it's the most honest I've been," Harry said.

"I've never written and recorded a song like that. The song at a time when any barrier of editing myself had been stripped away. I never do anything while listening to it, it's a song that makes me stop and listen rather than doing something and having it on in the background."

While Harry has a few songwriting credits to his name during his time in 1D, including 'Olivia', 'Stockholm Syndrome' and 'Happily', it wasn't until he left that band that Harry had the time to sit down and really work on complete song stories, not just fragments. "At certain times, you write songs where you just want to tell the whole story," he says. With 1D, "we were touring all the time," he remembered. "I wrote more as we went, especially on the last two albums. But I think it was tough to really delve in and find out who you are as a writer when you're just kind of dipping your toe each time. We didn't get the six months to see what kind of shit you can work with. To have time to live with a song, see what you love as a fan, chip at it, hone it and go for that ... it's heaven."

# "In the least weird way possible, my album is my favourite album to listen to at the moment."

**Right:** Man in Black – Harry visits *Elvis Duran and the Morning Show* at Z100 Studio on July 19, 2017, in New York City.

Harry wanted to spend time on a song, and explore why a particular set of lyrics tumbled out of his head. He also wanted to push boundaries within himself and to confound expectations of what his fans, and critics, might expect from his debut album. It was a nerve-wracking experience. But a learning curve too. "I've never felt this vulnerable putting out music, because I don't think this is a piece of myself I've put out there before. And, simple fact: When there are other people around you, you share the good stuff – but you also get to share the bad stuff and hide behind everyone else a little bit. So, with this, yeah, it is scary. But I think it was time for me to be scared. And I'm still very much learning. And I'm having the time of my life working this out."

Choosing the final 10 songs from a selection of 70 proved to be Harry's greatest challenge, and one that required him to step back and accept constructive criticism, a hard thing to do. "If you write a song that's personal to you, it's tough to hand that over to a band. It's so much easier saying something to an instrument than it is to a person. The guys that I was working with, we were kind of all working it out together. But in terms of choosing the songs and the track listing, it was probably time for me to have to make some decisions for myself and not be able to hide behind anyone else." That said, Harry did reach out to one person for his thoughts on the album's final track listing. He called his old friend, Ed Sheeran. It's his honest opinion that Harry has sought since the earliest days of 1D. "I played Ed a couple of songs after the album was finished," he revealed.

**Above:** SiriusXM fans get the full Styles show at the Roxy Theatre, California, May 17, 2017.

**Right:** Rehearsing for his *The One Show* at BBC Studios, London, May 12, 2017.

**Overleaf:** Jeff Bhasker, Harry, and director Cameron Crowe wow the crowd at LA'S GRAMMY Museum, September 15, 2017.

"He liked one that wasn't on there, so I did have a bit of a minute of, 'Oh no!', but if you start asking too many people, it gets away from what you like."

With the album finished and the track listing chosen, the finished product was complete. *Harry Styles* was ready for the world to hear. Harry was delighted with the album, and so were other people. Jeff Bhasker, was pleased with its star too. "I'm so proud of the album itself, and also of Harry for being so brave, and committing 100 per cent, and writing the kind of vulnerable lyrics that he wrote, and not pandering to what people thought he would do. People have no idea that this is what Harry Styles is like. Just like I didn't know. He's obviously very famous and beloved,

but people don't know the depths of what an amazing personality and artist he is."

Jeff wasn't alone in his positive reaction. An excited Harry gathered his family together for a first listen and was keen to hear their honest feedback. "My mum liked it, which was handy," he claimed, adding: "I played it to the family for the first time and there's one song on the album where there's a bit with a vocal effect on it. The whole album finished, then my stepdad said: 'I've one question, where did you get the duck from, how did you get a duck in the studio?' I was like: 'That was me, thanks.'"

The critical reaction to the album was also largely positive. And the reaction from his fans was overwhelmingly positive. Knowing that every lyric and chord change would be dissected ("which is amazing, that people care enough about you to try and figure out what it means"), and overanalyzed was something Harry had come to expect from One Direction releases.

"

I like to separate my personal life and work. It helps, I think, for me to compartmentalize. It's not about trying to make my career longer, like I'm trying to be this 'mysterious character', because I'm not. When I go home, I feel like the same person I was at school. You can't expect to keep that if you show everything. There's the work and the personal stuff, and going between the two is my favourite shit. It's amazing to me.

"

However, now that he was on his own, the album's worldwide reaction was something that weighed heavily on his mind.

As the May release date approached, it's clear he had some nerves: "This record made me really happy to make, so to a certain degree that feels very much like the reward. I definitely hope that people like it, it's something that I'm really proud of. I think in terms of the sound, it was my first album, so going into the process I didn't know what my solo album sounded like. So, I think during the process, there is a lot of different stuff that happened and the album reflects that. There's a lot of different stuff on there and I think I wanted whoever listens to it to kind of go with the process of finding my way and learning with me."

The first half of 2017 was a frightening, yet defining, time for the young artist still trying to find his feet, despite having sold millions of albums already. "I mean, I've never done this before. I don't know what the fuck I'm doing. I'm happy I found this band and these musicians, where you can be vulnerable enough to put yourself out there. I'm still learning … but it's my favourite lesson. If all I get is to make this music, I'm content. If I'm never on that big ride again, I'm happy and proud of it."

On its release, *Harry Styles* achieved the highest first sales week for a British male artist's debut full-length album since 1991, so the singer's millions of fans can look forward to hearing more of his songs and how he really feels for many years to come. But, it's worth remembering that Harry also halted the writing and recording process to go and spend six months getting wet off the western French Coast, being thrown about as Alex, a young private in Christopher Nolan's Oscar-winning Second World War drama *Dunkirk*. As if making his first solo album was not challenge enough, he was now acting for the first time, and in a Hollywood blockbuster, which goes to show just how much of an extraordinary talent Harry is. How many other artists of his age juggle two massive projects at the same time, and come out the other end in one piece?

Let's be clear about this: *Dunkirk* was not a low-budget, indie rom-com about a 20-something hipster struggling to make sense of the world, the kind of film you might expect a superstar in Harry's position to make in order to break into the film industry. No, Harry's first film was a multi-million-dollar epic, a saga told in three separate timelines by Christopher Nolan, one of Hollywood's leading auteur directors.

> "My first day on set was so cold, there was sand in my eyes, it was intense. The movie is really ambitious."

As ever, Harry defies convention – and blows all expectations out of the water.

But let's rewind to the first quarter to 2016. It was then that Harry, freshly released from his One Direction responsibilities, heard of a casting for Nolan's new film. He had to try, right? "I auditioned and I guess got it," Harry said, rather nonchalantly. "I am a massive fan of Chris Nolan's movies and I think it's something that I would be very excited to watch had I not been involved in it. It was pretty amazing to get to be part of the process. He never makes you feel like you have to try too hard. He wants it to be like you're saying stuff for the first time and doing stuff for the first time – because you are."

*Dunkirk* is the true story of the evacuation of Allied forces from the French town of Dunkirk, and their escape from the Nazi armies. The nine-day siege of the town saw the evacuation of almost 400,000 soldiers from the beaches of Dunkirk, though many soldiers and civilians lost their lives too. Christopher Nolan's film is the harrowing retelling of one of the war's darkest moments – when simply getting the hell out of somewhere alive could be seen as a victory.

**Right:** Harry with his other "Moles", film producer Emma Nolan and director Christopher Nolan in Dunkirk to promote *Dunkirk*.

"

The scale of the production was very overwhelming. I think whatever you imagine kind of a giant film set to be like, this was very ambitious even by those standards. You know the boats and the planes and the volume of bodies … it was pretty amazing.

"

The film gives us three perspectives – from the land, from the sea and from the sky.

Harry Styles was cast by Christopher Nolan in 2015 to play Alex, a private in the Argyll and Sutherland Highlanders, a regiment of the British Army. In order to land the part, Harry cut off his shoulder-length trademark hair. It was reported that Harry won the role after auditioning against hundreds of candidates and that Nolan was unaware of Styles' level of fame as a singer before casting him. Harry got the part on his talents, not his fame. In an interview to promote the film, Nolan explained: "I don't think I was that aware really of how famous Harry was. I mean, my daughter had talked about him. My kids talked about him, but I wasn't really that aware of it. So, the truth is, I cast Harry because he fit the part wonderfully and truly earned a seat at the table. When I cast Heath Ledger as the Joker in *The Dark Knight*, it raised a lot of eyebrows and caused a lot of comment. I have to trust my instincts, and Harry was perfect for this part."

With the director in Harry's corner and praising his acting ability since his first screen test, the singer was able to commit 110 per cent to the role, allowing him the freedom to break free from the chains of Harry Styles the Pop Star. "What I was seeing when Harry auditioned was a very charismatic guy who clearly had a truthfulness and a subtlety in his ability to perform as a film actor."

The filming process was often challenging and difficult, and it threw the multi-millionaire pop star completely out of his comfort zone. "The movie is so ambitious. Some of the stuff they're doing in this movie is insane. And it was hard, man, physically really tough, but I love acting. I love playing someone else. I'd sleep really well at night, then get up and continue drowning." Harry's character, Alex, is one of the lead roles on the scenes on the Mole, one of the jetties of Dunkirk that suffered a week-long tirade of punishing air and land assaults by the Nazis, who had by that time occupied most of France. The film has many standout scenes of derring-do and bravery in the face of overwhelming adversity, and Harry's Alex is one of the underdogs the audiences hopes to see return home.

There were set pieces that put shivers down Harry's spine. And that's saying something considering he has performed in front of millions of people. "There was one day when we were filming, where we were swimming nearby one of the larger boats – I think that was the day there was the most number of things going crazy.

There was a boat blowing up as you were swimming, there were bullet noises everywhere, there was fire, people screaming and cameramen screaming ... There was a lot going on. There was a bit where you're like, are we filming? What just happened?"

Another day on set saw one of Harry's favourite moments when the director poked fun at the "inexperienced actor turned pop star" – a man who has had more camera close-ups than many experienced actors over a lifetime of acting. "In terms of first-day memories," Harry said, "we finished one shot and he said, 'Congrats on your first close-up!'"

**Above:** Harry arrives at the *Dunkirk* world premiere at London's Odeon Leicester Square, July 13, 2017.

Harry may have had very few lines to learn – there are only a few hundred words spoken in the entire film – but the role required acting that was physically demanding, requiring the nuances of body language. The fear had to be real in the eyes of the actors, and the emotion transmitted had to be genuine. "Chris creates this worldview where you don't have to act that much," Harry said. "He tries to make it so he is capturing natural reactions to stuff. I think as hard as it would ever be on set, everyone was very aware of how, in comparison to what obviously people would have been through, this was nothing. We got to go home and shower at the end of the day. That obviously makes it much easier to deal with."

Shooting the film on the Mole with the other young actors in the film, including Fionn Whitehead and Tom Glynn-Carney, created a brotherly bond on set and was a positive and enriching experience for the young actor. "I feel lucky to be involved in it. Chris has an amazing brain, the way he works stuff out. He clearly does so much research and I guess that's why he doesn't just churn out a load of movies. It definitely takes some of the nerves away – you know if you do something wrong he'll tell you."

Harry's best friend and One Direction bandmate Niall Horan was supportive from the start. "I'll tell you what, if Christopher Nolan takes you on, you must be a good actor," he enthused. "I'm looking forward to seeing Dunkirk, it's going to be an unbelievable movie, but when one of your mates is in it, then it's going to be even better. I think Harry is going to do well. I'd imagine he was pretty nervous to cut his hair off. He spent about two years growing that so I wouldn't say he was very happy about that ... but he's in a movie now!"

**Left:** Harry as Alex in a famous scene from the movie Dunkirk.

"**"We're not trying to oversell Harry in the movie for the specific reason that it's an ensemble. We don't want people who are huge fans of his being disappointed that he's not in it enough or whatever."**

CHRISTOPHER NOLAN

His performance was overwhelmingly well received. Costar Jack Lowden, who plays RAF pilot Collins, enjoyed his costar's screen debut performance. "It's admirable that the guy's having a pop, I guess he's today's equivalent of a Beatle. I think he got on well. That man knows what he's doing." Chris Nolan, also, spoke out at how well Harry got on. "I think what he does is extremely subtle because it's very real," Nolan said. "It's not cartoonish. His performance almost risks being missed because of what it's actually doing."

For Harry, it was a rewarding experience, and a fun distraction from his day job, but he may not be aching to act again. "I feel I may have peaked too soon in many ways. I was pretty tired afterwards. It might be one and done for me, but I'd do this one again for sure!"

With *Dunkirk* a critical and commercial hit in the summer, as well as his debut album sailing effortlessly to the top of the charts, 2017 was a stellar year for the singer. This was his solo moment in the spotlight and he wasn't going to waste a second. It came as no surprise, then, that as *Harry Styles* was riding high in the charts, Harry the man announced a string of tour dates – his first ever headline show.

Kicking off live and loud in September 2017, Harry's Live On Tour tour may not have been as big or as extensive as those he enjoyed while a member of 1D or his subsequent Love On Tour, but it was more in keeping with the emerging solo artist.

**Right:** The iHeartRadio album release party for Harry Styles saw the man in question perform the album in its entirety, May 8, 2017.

A solo artist who wants to have a more intimate experience with his fans. Suffice to say the tour sold out in seconds, prompting Harry to beam proudly on Twitter: "I am overwhelmed, thank you.

If I don't get to see you this tour, I'll come back around next year if you'll have me. Love, H."

Starting in San Francisco, California at The Masonic Theatre and concluding nine months later at Los Angeles' iconic Forum arena, Live On Tour took in 88 shows across more than 25 countries across South America, Europe, North America, Asia, and Australia and New Zealand. It was a world away from his touring days with his former group. "The first few gigs we ever did as One Direction, in some nightclubs, girls were fainting and getting pulled out of the audience. We thought it was the strangest thing we ever saw. I didn't think any of us would get used to the screaming, and that reaction. It's just mad." Now, with his fans grown up alongside their favourite singer, Harry doubts that girls will be fainting at his solo shows, but hopes that they keep on singing: "Honestly, I think it is as simple as it's my first tour, it's my first album and I'm looking forward to playing these songs to people. I think it's appropriate, I guess. I think they will be fun, it's always nice to be able to have a lot of energy in those venues and I'm excited to play the venues – the venues are amazing places. I don't think it's like a super deliberate thing, but I think I really wanted to go out and play the new songs for some fans who wanted to come watch and I think it's going to be cool."

While Harry's six-piece band had a selection of 70 solo songs to choose from, including the 10 choice cuts that made up the debut album, fans were relieved to hear that Harry was also playing one or two 1D songs in the set list as the tour progressed into arena shows in 2018. "At first, he was definitely cautiously up for it," Tom Hull said of the decision to play 'What Makes You Beautiful' on the solo tour. "I feel like those One Direction songs are brilliantly written songs, and obviously it was a moment where we had a conversation. Beyoncé does Destiny's Child songs, so we were like 'Let's do some of the songs that people will all know and everyone will love.'" Harry might have been on board to perform 1D's first, and perhaps biggest hit, but rather than just regurgitate the recorded version of the song, he wanted to adapt the tune to fit in with the rest of set, giving it a "Ray Charles-y vibe" with a "Motown-y beat". "We all

have so much respect for what put him here," Hull explained, adding: "It's an important part of it. You can't underestimate his fans."

Other songs that made the live show were 'Story of my Life' and the song that Harry wrote for Ariana Grande in 2014, 'Just a Little Bit of your Heart'. Hull explained: "Bands become true bands on tour. Fans bought tickets [for this tour] before the album had come out, and the band wants to play to them. The idea is to cut our chops on this tour and get really good. Then next year, he's got an arena tour. It's quite good to be able to do Harry's record and have other songs in the set because he's written so much music with and outside of One Direction. We're presenting it in a way that sort of reflects the record and where he's at now, which feels unique to Harry."

The tour was in full swing, he had a number one solo album, acting credibility in a blockbuster film, and huge personal wealth, life for Harry Styles was looking good. At that time, there was just one final thing that would make Harry's life complete, something that takes us back to the first page of this book – this idea of family, the largest piece in the puzzle of Harry's life. The idea of Harry starting his own family crops up every now and again, and sends his large female fanbase into overdrive. As Harry enters into the second chapter of his life, it seems that baby-making is somewhere high up on his priority list. "I'm feeling quite broody. I can't wait. I don't mean right now, I mean. When I eventually have kids, that's something I'm looking forward. For now, I feel like you enjoy experiences more when you go with people you really want to be with and really care about." But as we found out, Harry Styles the solo artist was just getting started.

**Left:** The opening tour date for his first solo headline tour began in San Francisco, California, at The Masonic, September 19, 2017.

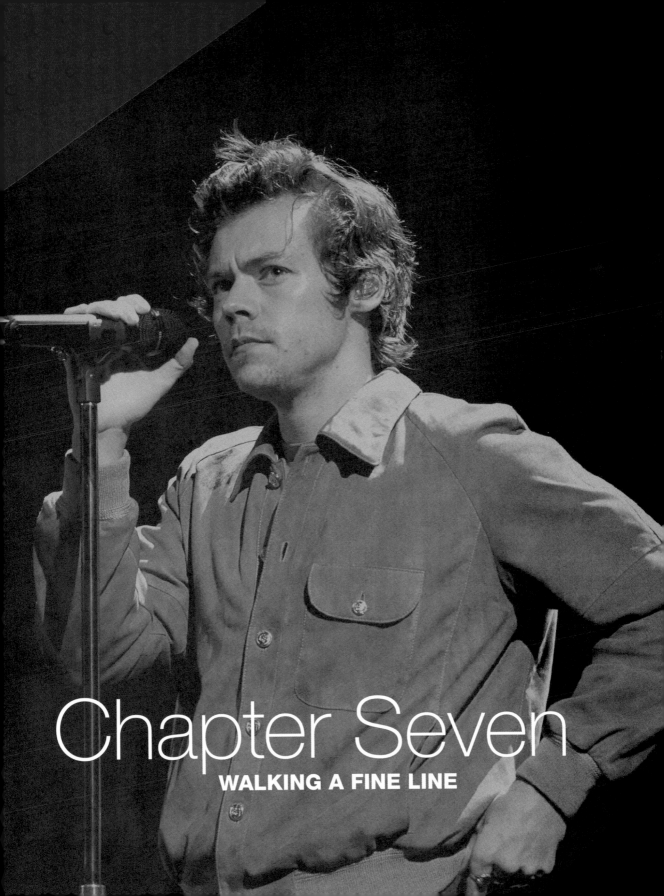

# Chapter Seven
## WALKING A FINE LINE

# WALKING A FINE LINE

THE TOUR TO SUPPORT HARRY STYLES THE ALBUM BEGAN IN 2017 AND IT WAS STILL GOING STRONG AT THE FINALE, IN JULY 2018 WITH TWO PACKED NIGHTS AT THE FORUM IN INGLEWOOD, CALIFORNIA. OVER THE TOUR, HARRY AND HIS BAND HAD PLAYED IN FRONT OF NEARLY ONE MILLION FANS ACROSS THE GLOBE AND HAD GARNERED SUPPORT EVERYWHERE THEY WENT. SUCH A SCHEDULE MAY HAVE PUT SOME YOUNG ARTISTS OFF, BUT HARRY WAS USED TO IT. OUTSIDE OF MUSIC AND EXPLORING HIS INTEREST IN FASHION, STYLES BECAME A MODEL FOR ITALIAN POWERHOUSE DESIGNER GUCCI, MAKING HEADLINES FOR HIS EVER MORE COLOURFUL COSTUMES. HAD THE CORONAVIRUS PANDEMIC NOT HIT, THERE'S NO KNOWING WHERE HARRY WOULD HAVE ENDED UP IN A SHORT SPACE OF TIME. AS IT WAS, THE ENFORCED REST SPURRED HIM INTO CREATIVE ENDEAVOURS ACROSS MULTIPLE DISCIPLINES ANYWAY – IT JUST TOOK HIM A LITTLE LONGER ...

Harry's first solo tour started brilliantly and he also picked up the Best International Artist award at the 2017 ARIA Music Awards in November. The tour ended well too, with many accolades and a huge number of satisfied fans all over the world, from San Francisco, California, where the tour started, to, err, Inglewood, California, where it ended. Although those two are less than 400 miles apart, Harry and the crew clocked up thousands of miles on their quest to entertain the world with music from the new album ... and a little bit more. On the 85 dates in between those two, the tour hit Europe, South America, Oceania and Asia. And as the student paper, the UCLA's student paper the *Daily Bruin* commented, "the singer has successfully shed his tween dreamboat persona and established himself as a musician worthy of serious consideration." And that was part of a crucial step for Harry that saw not just a boost in confidence as

a presenter and performer, but also as a songwriter and celebrity. Playing between 14 and 17 songs, the setlist evolved through the five months the band was on the road (excluding the break of January to March 2018). One Direction songs were usually featured in the performance, the most popular being 'Stockholm Syndrome' and 'What Makes You Beautiful', and a few other covers besides. Regularly making up the encore was Fleetwood Mac's 'The Chain'. Styles had made friends with the Mac's Stevie Nicks a few years previously, and Harry even brought the singer a cake for her birthday (he did work as a baker previously you recall ...). Prior to the Live On Tour concerts, Harry had shared a stage with Nicks in 2017 when they

**Left:** Harry at the ARIA Awards on November 28, 2017 in Sydney, Australia, where he scooped the Best International Artist award.

played 'Two Ghosts' and 'Landslide' together, Styles introduced her by saying, "If there was any doubt, I'm pretty sure I'd like to confirm, in my entire life, I never thought I'd be able to say this ... Please welcome to the stage, Stevie Nicks." This was at the legendary Troubadour club – one of the world's all time great rock venues – so you can understand why Harry was so excited. Nicks returned the favour in January 2018, when Harry played 'The Chain' with Fleetwood Mac at the 2018 MusiCares Person of the Year Awards. Harry again introduced the band, stating, "There are several things I thought I would never be doing in my life. One is sharing the stage with these legends ... let alone having the honor of introducing them to the stage." In 2019, Nicks famously called Harry "The son I never had," in an interview with *Rolling Stone* magazine, even referring to him as her and Mick Fleetwood's "love child". Having rock royalty such as Nicks on board is no surprise to regular Styles followers, however. And when Nicks was inducted into the Rock and Roll Hall of Fame as a solo artist, Styles was the man for the job; they performed 'Stop Draggin' My Heart Around' – the duet made famous by Stevie Nicks and Tom Petty – to much acclaim. To cap it all, Nicks performed with Styles in 2019 at The Forum.

In terms of appearance, Styles was further evolving his flamboyant character aspects with his clothes, his demeanour and his public persona. In an interview with actor Timothée Chalamet that Styles undertook for *ID Magazine* in 2018, the two discussed fashion, films, masculinity and appearance – among other things. Harry said of the last of those, "I think if you stay in that safe space all the time, it's very easy to get bored." And his actions spoke as loud as his words, as he wore ever more colourful and gender-challenging outfits. Later that year, Harry undertook some modelling work for Italian powerhouse of fashion Gucci, fronting a campaign and demonstrating his professionalism in front of a lens yet again. Harry kept this up consistently, and was involved in the New

**Left:** Harry the 2019 Met Gala in New York. Decked out in Gucci and ready for the upcoming exhibition Camp: Notes on Fashion.

**Right:** Harry playing his famous 'End Gun Violence' guitar, on stage at New York's Madison Square Garden, June 2018.

**Overleaf:** Harry Styles and Stevie Nicks on stage at the 2019 Rock and Roll Hall of Fame induction ceremony for Nicks as a solo artist.

York Metropolitan Museum of Art's 2019 exhibition entitled Camp: Notes on Fashion. At the associated Met Gala benefit, he appeared dressed in Gucci, with other co-chairs including Lady Gaga, Serena Williams and Alessandro Michele.

But music was what Harry stuck to most in the months after his first solo tour success, and he was already busy on solo album number two, *Fine Line*. In order to understand that album, we need to take a quick peek into Harry's private life. Harry famously had a relationship with French–American model Camille Rowe that lasted for around a year; the break-up coming pretty much at the same time as his

tour end in 2018. The couple originally met through mutual friend and fellow model Alexa Chung and it seemed things were serious. However, it was not to be and the relationship fell by the wayside quite suddenly. Another older woman for Harry, Camille has modelled for various big names and turned out to be a huge influence on his songwriting. In *Rolling Stone*, Harry's BFF Tom Hull revealed that the couple's breakup, "had a big impact on [Styles]". In that same interview, Harry opened up about the crossover from his personal life into his songwriting: "for me, music is where I let that cross over. It's the only place, strangely, where it feels right to let that cross over." It turned out that many of the songs on *Fine Line* were inspired by this relationship, the most blatantly obvious in the song 'Cherry', which includes a sample from a voicemail – reportedly from Rowe – at the end.

Towards the end of the process of making the album, in August 2019, Harry described it as being about

**Left:** Harry's tearful performance at the 2020 BRITs in London, a few days after the sudden death of his ex-girlfriend Caroline Flack.

**Below:** December 2020, and Harry's shows in Inglewood, California are announced; they eventually took place in November.

"having sex and feeling sad," indicating once again the personal nature of many of the songs. It was Hull, long-time collaborator with Styles, who encouraged him to deal with his feelings through music. And in a deviation from his usual clean-living tendencies, Styles also reported biting his tongue while "doing mushrooms," and singing with blood in his mouth.

The recording process was smooth though, and much of the team from his first album *Harry Styles* was reunited. Hull was more involved with the production this time around, with Tyler Johnson also producing and collaborating with Harry more than on that first solo album. The musical core of Johnson, Hull, Mitch Rowland and Jeff Bhasker was present again – a group of musicians very familiar with each other. There was a bigger cast of other contributors, with string musicians, vocalists and more guests besides.

A more self-reflective but fun album than his debut, *Fine Line* has a more mellow vibe, taking inspiration from such 1960s artists as Van Morrison and Joni Mitchell. Styles even cited the legendary albums *Astral Weeks* and *Blue* from each artist respectively. He told *Rolling Stone*'s Rob Sheffield that he was so obsessed by the dulcimer sound from Mitchell's album that he traced the woman who had built the instrument used on it. She subsequently gifted Harry a dulcimer, and "gave us a lesson ... we were all jamming with these big Cheshire Cat grins," he said.

*Fine Line* was released shortly before Christmas in 2019, although singles 'Lights Up' and 'Adore You' both came out beforehand, in October and December respectively.

Described as a pop record by most, *Fine Line* is a solid offering that went down well with critics, fans and

**Above:** Harry at the Grammy Awards in March 2021, where he won the Best Pop Solo Performance for 'Watermelon Sugar'.

award givers alike. It was an instant success stateside, going straight to the top of the *Billboard* 200 in the USA in its first week, making Harry Styles the first UK male artist to debut at number one with their first two albums. Followers of Harry since his early days were not surprised in the least – even when part of One Direction it was clear that Harry was good at surrounding himself with talented people and inspiring them. The only question was whether Harry could come up with his own material on a regular basis; *Fine Line* answered that question convincingly once and for all, as Harry is the writer of every single one of the 12 songs on the album. Seven of them were released as singles at various times, further testament to the young man's skills in a studio. Back home (well, sometimes) in the UK, the album reached number three initially, peaked at number two, but failed to dislodge Harry's friend Taylor Swift from the top spot.

The album was, however, a steady seller in Harry's home country, reaching platinum status. Elsewhere, *Fine Line* was a resounding global hit, reaching the top spot in many countries, including Argentina, Australia, Mexico and Canada. Critics were favourable too, his songwriting maturity coming in for praise in the *Guardian*, saying that he is "taking his time coming into focus." *Pitchfork* was less complimentary, but still recognized "glimpses ... of the sort of intimate connection Styles hopes to forge." *Rolling Stone* joined the 4/5 review bandwagon, calling the album "a streamlined, party-ready, primary-colors take on the enduring concept of the rock & roll starman" and, significantly, saying "if there's a nontoxic masculinity, Harry Styles just might've found it."

This last quote, coming from a single, male musician in the #MeToo era should be taken as a huge compliment. Alongside the movies, the music industry has far to go to clean up its act regarding equal rights and fair treatment for many, women in particular. Singling Styles out in this positive manner is, beyond a throwaway line at the end of a music review, a worthy plaudit for the young man, who has always worked hard with his fair treatment message. As we have seen, way back in 2012, Harry was supportive of women, and his female fans. Later, when Emma Watson gave a powerful speech on gender equality, Harry was one celebrity swift to voice his support. Further, in 2019 he said, "I think there's so much masculinity in being vulnerable and allowing yourself to be feminine, and I'm very comfortable with that."

Almost precisely one month before the album dropped, the announcement came that there would be a tour in support. Love On Tour would be a bigger deal than the one in support of debut album *Harry Styles*. That had been a great success, with sellouts and rave reviews aplenty. But this time the scope was different; nobody was worried about Harry and the band's ability to deliver – and deliver big. For his new musical vibe, arenas were the ideal size – including multiple nights at New York's legendary Madison Square Garden – and there were plenty of stadiums and other large venues booked all around the world.

During a chat about 'Lights Out' from *Fine Line*, Harry himself spoke about prospects of a tour on London's Capital Radio. He said that it may take place in 2020 ("I wanna tour next year, maybe, don't know, potentially, maybe not – haven't announced that yet"). So, expectation was high that it would be a big deal, and the official announce boasted 26 dates across Europe, then a three-week break before starting again in Philadelphia, USA. Harry even hosted *Saturday Night Live* as well as performing on it to promote the tour. The future was looking so bright. But then ... Covid.

In 2020, no sooner had the announcement gone out that Harry Styles would take part in the annual Wango Tango concert in the US as part of his tour, it was announced that the concert was cancelled; and a

## TRACKLISTING
*What's your* Fine Line *favourite?*

'Golden'
'Watermelon Sugar'
'Adore You'
'Lights Up'
'Cherry'
'Falling'
'To Be So Lonely'
'She'
'Sunflower, Vol. 6'
'Canyon Moon'
'Treat People With Kindness'
'Fine Line'

> **"** You open a bunch of doors in your house that you didn't know existed, you find all these rooms and you get to explore them. **"**

HARRY ON THERAPY

few short months after the big announce of his global tour had gone out, Love On Tour 2020 was postponed until 2021. And so the world sank into the hiatus that was the global Coronavirus pandemic.

Harry stayed busy (would he ever have been able to take a break?); his phrase 'Treat People With Kindness' was seen on a charity t-shirt again (previously used on two Pride shirts), this time with the slogan STAY HOME. STAY SAFE. PROTECT EACH OTHER. All proceeds went to charity.

Most of the world went into lockdown, Harry too, and he stated to Fenn O'Meally on 1Xtra radio, "It's a little difficult but it's all right." He continued, "I'm lucky I'm with friends in our little safe self-isolation pod." He added, "Now is the perfect time to learn a new skill or try a new hobby or something, right?" And he took the pandemic seriously, telling MTV, "There's hundreds of people dying every day." But in a quote that made his fans even happier than ever, he said, "I think a lot of powerful music is going to come from that [pandemic]." And Harry's lucky fans were going to find out just how much shortly after the world got moving again in the wake of the devastating virus.

Harry was out on tour as soon as possible, and his postponed dates in the US were the first to happen. That series of concerts started on September 4, 2021 in Las Vegas, in front of 13,000 lucky fans. The original schedule was rendered patchy due to coronavirus rules, but in the end the full complement of concerts went ahead, in the US at least. Playing with restrictions made it a tough three months, but the band saw it through and fans rallied around, eager and thoroughly excited to be out in the world, let alone in a room with Harry Styles and his talented group of live musicians.

Back in the UK, Harry's songwriting prowess was rewarded with a win at the prestigious Ivor Novello Awards. The 2021 PRS For Music Most Performed went to 'Adore You' from *Fine Line*, which was penned by Harry, Amy Allen, Taylor Johnson and Kid Harpoon

(Harry's mate Tom). The award was extra sweet, coming only a few short years after Britpop legend Noel Gallagher complimented the awards, stating his appreciation, "because clowns like One Direction aren't invited." That was certainly a victory for Harry and the team, although worry about what Noel Gallagher thought was probably far from his mind.

That was not the only award Harry would pick up in 2021, for his style as well as his music: 'Watermelon Sugar' won the Best Pop Solo Performance category at the Grammys, and Harry was there to perform on the night. That same song was named British Single of the Year at the 2021 BRIT Awards, while 'Golden' was named Global Hit of the Year at the MTV Millennial Awards, and 'Treat People With Kindness' won the Best Choreography gong at the MTV Video Music Awards. Harry won Best Male at the 2021 Global Awards, rounding off yet another spectacular year for the young, hardworking musician. He was nominated for many others, and no more than his obvious talent, dedication and thoughtfulness deserved. Despite everything, 2021 was a year of success for Harry, and although the pandemic affected his touring considerably, he shone through and – as with so much in his life – was able to thrive, bring people together and unite his fans. But as the pandemic crisis waned, what would the next steps be for Harry? With the world at his feet, would it be a well-deserved rest? A further foray into fashion? More movies? As it would turn out, probably a little bit of all those things ...

**Previous spread:** October 31 (left) and 30 (right), 2021 and Harry – with a variety of colourful costumes – at his 'Harryween' party. Fans were encouraged to join in with the dressing up.

**Right:** Harry meets Marvel: Eros, played by Harry, was introduced to the millions of Marvel Cinematic Universe fans in 2021.

EROS

MARVEL STUDIOS
ETERNALS
ONLY IN THEATERS NOW
IN ◼◼Dolby Cinema. REAL D 3D AND IMAX

# Chapter Eight

## WELCOME TO HARRY'S HOUSE

# WELCOME TO HARRY'S HOUSE

GIVEN AN ENFORCED REST FROM TOURING AND MIXING WITH OTHER MUSICIANS IN PERSON, IT WAS NO SURPRISE THAT HARRY WORKED HARD, HONING HIS ALREADY FORMIDABLE SONGWRITING SKILLS. HIS THIRD SOLO ALBUM, *HARRY'S HOUSE*, WAS THE FRUIT OF THE SINGER'S LABOURS DURING 2020 AND 2021 – YEARS THAT WERE MUCH DISRUPTED FROM THE USUAL. HOWEVER, HARRY HAS CONTINUED TO ACHIEVE SO MUCH ACROSS SO MANY DISCIPLINES IT'S HARD TO SAY WHAT A USUAL YEAR LOOKS LIKE ON PLANET HARRY! BUT SONGWRITING AND PERFORMANCE ARE WHAT DRIVES HIM BEYOND ANYTHING ELSE, AND THE NEW DECADE HAD STARTED WELL. TOWARDS THE END OF THE PANDEMIC, HARRY HAD ALREADY FINISHED ONE MAJOR TOUR AND WAS PREPARING FOR THE NEXT – OSTENSIBLY THE SECOND PART OF 2020'S POSTPONED LOVE ON TOUR. NEW CONCERTS WOULD PROVIDE THE IDEAL OPPORTUNITY TO SHOW OFF NEW MUSIC TO HIS FANS, OLD AND NEW ALIKE...

Towards the end of 2021, Harry had found the time to launch his own cosmetics brand, called Pleasing. It was another project that had been birthed during the pandemic and that saw light at the end of it. Styles said, "It was a fun little project, but during the pandemic, and when we eventually named it Pleasing, it felt like it was so much more than nail polish." As you would imagine from someone as thoughtful and scrupulous as Harry, the cosmetics are all cruelty free, vegan and made with ethically sourced material. It is yet another example of how Styles is able to apply himself across many different areas, and because he is conscientious and careful, he tends towards success in whichever he turns his hand to.

As soon as he was able, Harry kept up with his acting career. In an interesting acting move, Harry landed the part of Jack Chambers in the American psychological thriller *Don't Worry Darling*, directed by Olivia Wilde. The movie is set in the 1950s. Apparently, romance blossomed in reality as well as on the screen, for Olivia and Harry were reputed to be dating, having met on the set of the movie. Olivia is outspoken on the subject of women's rights so the pair would have some things in common, and the age difference – ten years – is something that Harry-followers have become used to; it seems Harry's maturity belies his age. Although the couple kept their relationship quiet on set, when they were pictured together at a wedding, the cat was truly out of the bag. The relationship developed quickly, and Wilde had admired Styles before – she "did a little victory dance" when he signed up officially for the

**Left:** Harry taking it easy as Spotify celebrate the record-breaking release of his third solo album, *Harry's House*, in May of 2022.

film, she told *People* magazine. Not long afterwards, the story of Wilde's formal split with the father of her two children was all over the media. Her partner was Jason Sudeikis, familiar to many as the creator and star of Apple TV's London-based football comedy drama and multiple award-winner, *Ted Lasso*.

When *Don't Worry Darling* wrapped, Wilde posted a fascinating paragraph on Instagram praising Styles, stating that, "not only did he relish the opportunity to allow for the brilliant @florencepugh [Florence Pugh] to hold center stage as our 'Alice', but he infused each scene with a nuanced sense of humanity." Suffice to say, Wilde and Styles made a great couple, and although Twitter was disappointed to learn that Harry was no longer single, the couple seemed genuinely happy and very much in love.

Following the filming of *Don't Worry Darling*, later in 2021 Harry was spotted in Brighton, England, on set in a drama named *My Policeman*, a movie adaptation of the Bethan Roberts novel that takes place in the 1950s – it seems that Harry has the kind of face and demeanour that suits period pieces – in

Britain's popular southern coastal town. True to type, Harry doesn't just involve himself in any old run-of-the-mill projects, and *My Policeman* is significant for the part he plays in a love triangle featuring two men and a woman. Harry's part is the policeman of the title, who, despite being married to a female school teacher, also enjoys a physical relationship with a man. The movie, produced by Amazon Studios, was made after Amazon snapped up the movie rights amid stiff competition. Lily James was originally rumoured to play the part of Harry's wife, but she was replaced by Emma Corrin, who is famous for playing the part of Prince Charles' first wife, Lady Diana Spencer, in the Netflix drama *The Crown*.

It was not until March of 2022 that Styles announced his third solo album, with the title *Harry's House*. He unveiled the artwork, a trailer and the release date, which was set as May 20, 2022. Joni Mitchell, one of the artist's biggest influences for his previous

---

**Above:** Harry on the set of *My Policeman* in Brighton, England, in May 2021 with co-star Emma Corrin.

Acting is kind of uncomfortable at times; you have to trust a lot ... Being able to trust your director is a gift, that was very helpful. It meant for a really nice experience working on that movie.

HARRY ON FILMING *DON'T WORRY DARLING*

album, was rendered happy by the title, revealing her enthusiasm on Twitter. Keen-eyed fans noted that there was a track on Mitchell's 1975 album *The Hissing of Summer Lawns* entitled 'Harry's House/Centerpiece'.

Harry moved quickly, and the first single from *Harry's House*, 'As It Was', came out a few weeks later, on April 1. The perfectly balanced pop tune shot straight to the top of the charts in both the USA and UK, making it his second solo number one single in both of those countries. It even managed to break Spotify's record for most-streamed song by a male artist in 24 hours, as it racked up more than 16 million streams in that short timeframe. Written by Harry himself and produced by long-time collaborators Tom Hull and Tyler Johnson, 'As It Was' was a chart-topper all over the world and further proof – if any was really needed – of Harry's ability to satisfy fans old and new, and to make new friends musically. The song marked a further departure from his more rock-based sounds, with a 1990s-edged pop beat. The accompanying video – dropped on the same day – was filmed in some

original London locations, including the Barbican Centre and the old London Zoo penguin enclosure! A colourful, sparkly treat, the video was made in February amid much speculation that new music from Harry was on the way. It was directed by Ukrainian film-maker Tanu Muino, who has shot for Yungblud, Post Malone and Lizzo, and who won the MTV Video Music Award for Best Direction with Lil Nas X for 'Montero (Call Me By Your Name)'. The video was as well received as the song, garnering much praise, with *Glamour* magazine writing, "the talents of Styles do not disappoint", although much attention was drawn to the Ukraimnian director's reaction to the invasion of her homeland by Russia, which occurred during the shoot for 'As It Was'. A consummate professional, she finished shooting.

When quizzed about the new album and its development during the Covid pandemic-inspired lockdowns, Styles told journalist Lou Stoppard, "I

**Above:** A very colourful Harry Styles accepting his prize for British Single at the 2021 BRIT Awards: 'Watermelon Sugar'.

think everyone went through a big moment of self-reflection, and I don't know if there's anything more navel-gazing than making an album." This carried on the narrative that *Harry's House* was to be even more introspective than his two previous solo albums. But Styles claimed he was happy with it just as it was: "it doesn't feel like my life is over if this album isn't a commercial success," he said, indicating that he felt less pressure upon the release of *Harry's House* than he had on the last two solo efforts.

One of the album's tracks, 'Boyfriends' dates back to the end of his *Fine Line* sessions, initially written in 2019. But *Harry's House* is a departure from that sound, and is a very new album in itself. 'Late Night Talking' was the second single from the album to be released, coming out in late May to more popular acclaim.

Again all the tracks – 13 this time – were penned by Harry himself, with his usual collaborators present. Amy Allen, with whom Harry shared the Ivor Novello

prize for 'Adore You' in 2021, was co-writer on the tear-jerking track 'Matilda'.

Positive reviews greeted the release, with the *Guardian* calling it "a mature third album where every song feels like a single" and even *Pitchfork* had to admit that "the album oozes the easy charisma that lifted Styles head and shoulders above his former One Direction colleagues and makes him one of pop's more compelling live acts." *Rolling Stone* namechecked Steely Dan, Al Green and Yo La Tengo, surely testament to Harry's now firmly established credentials as a serious artist. "This is a Santa Ana summer breeze of a record," their review concluded. *NME* acknowledged the introspective aspect of the album, stating how it is an "exploration of his definition of home". Harry himself returned to the introspective nature of the album as well as touching on his appreciation for others in an interview with NPR's Leila Fadel for the show *Morning Edition*: "While this is such a personal album, and so much about my own journey finding a place of home, I also feel like it's very much dedicated to my friends," he told the journalist, but hinted that

**Above:** Billboards in New York's Times Square herald the release of the singer's third solo album, *Harry's House*, in May 2022.

# "Coachella, each and every single one of you thank you so so much. Life is all about moments, and this is one I will not forget."

## TRACKLISTING
*Harry's House*

'Music For A Sushi Restaurant'
'Late Night Talking'
'Grapejuice'
'As It Was'
'Daylight'
'Little Freak'
'Matilda'
'Cinema'
'Daydreaming'
'Keep Driving'
'Satellite'
'Boyfriends'
'Love of My Life'

there is more to come from his personal development as well as his music, as he is still figuring out some of life's bigger questions: "I think getting to a place where I feel like, 'This is what I do and I love it, but it's not necessarily who I am' just feels like a much healthier place to be operating from and making music from."

The record features the same core of musicians and producers as *Fine Line*, with Tom Hull (as Kid Harpoon), Tyler Johnson and Mitch Rowland taking centre stage with Harry. And as is now common on a Harry Styles record, there is also a group of talented musicians contributing here and there across various tracks. The legendary singer-songwriter and Grammy award-winner Ben Harper even turns up playing slide guitar on 'Boyfriends'.

Marketing and publicity exploded around the album release, with pop-up shops appearing in Los Angeles, New York and London. On sale were branded clothes, music, posters, 'Treat People With Kindness' water bottles and plenty more. It was certainly everything the Harry Styles fan could ask for, bar a personal appearance perhaps ... And for some lucky fans it had the potential to turn into a personal appearance, as tickets to sold-out concerts were given away to a select bunch of very lucky individuals. Single-night performances in London's Brixton Academy and New York's UBS Arena were on offer, and during those concerts Harry gave his all for what was labelled Harry Styles: One Night Only, and which served as a live introduction to *Harry's House* the album.

**Previous page:** Harry enjoying himself at Coachella 2022 in Indio, California, April 2022 where he was the headline act.

**Above:** Marketing for Harry's Fall tour in 2022 was huge, with no stone seemingly unturned, as this California street art shows.

**Left:** Harry, in a highly original outfit, performing for the *Today* TV show Summer Concert Series in New York City in May 2022.

**Overleaf:** Just before the European leg of Love On Tour, Harry played BBC Radio 1's Big Weekend in Coventry, May 29, 2022.

# "The crowd is so emotionally generous that they just want me to be having a good time, and I can feel that. Doing shows is my favourite thing to do in the world."

Harry's love of performing was clear in April 2022 when he performed at Coachella, headlining and performing three tracks from the new album: 'As It Was', 'Boyfriends', and 'Late Night Talking' – the latter two unreleased at the time of the concert.

Harry even got together with friend James Corden, host of the hugely popular and influential *The Late Late Show* in the US, to make a video for a third track on the album, the song 'Daylight'. Filmed by the two during a "drop-in" of a fan's flat, it had borrowed props, makeshift locations and costumes from anywhere, a long way from Harry's usual high budget videos. *Harry's House* stormed to number one across the world, hitting the top spot in the UK and US straight away, and the album outsold *Fine Line* in the US, making it Harry's biggest solo album to date. Also notable in the US was that four tracks from the album reached the top 10 of the *Billboard* Hot 100 at the same time: 'Late Night Talking', 'Music For A Sushi Restaurant', 'Matilda', and 'As It Was'. Harry became the first British solo artist to achieve this feat, with only the Beatles doing so before as a group, in 1964.

With all the publicity, marketing and buzz surrounding the album, the fact that Harry's tour was about to get going only led to a further frenzy of stories on social media, with excited fans more than ready to get behind the singer and cheer him along on his epic world tour. The European leg of Love On Tour formally kicked off in Scotland at the Ibrox Stadium in Glasgow on June 11, before Harry and the team headed down to London's Wembley Stadium for four epic nights in England's capital city.

Entertaining a stadium crowd is no problem for Harry – he's now been doing it almost longer than he hasn't, and his knack for communication and his flair for performance ensure that every concert he does is memorable for his adoring fan community. As he told Zane Lowe in an intimate 2022 interview, "The crowd is so emotionally generous that they just want me to be having a good time, and I can feel that. Doing shows is my favourite thing to do in the world." And may he never stop. Judging by the sell-out stadiums around the world, I don't think that is going to be likely!

**Right:** BBC Radio 1's Big Weekend festival was a two-dayer, with Harry Styles headlining on the Sunday.

# Credits

The publishers would like to thank the following sources for their kind permission to reproduce the pictures in this book.

4. Kevin Winter/Getty Images, 6. Jo Davidson/SHM/REX/Shutterstock, 7. Jon Furniss/WireImage/Getty Images, 10. Mike Marsland/WireImage/Getty Images, 11. David M. Benett/Dave Benett/Getty Images for Dazed, 12. Paul Lewis/REX/Shutterstock, 13. (left) Richard Young/REX/Shutterstock, (right) McPix Ltd/REX/Shutterstock, 14-15. McPix Ltd/REX/Shutterstock, 16. Beretta/Sims/REX/Shutterstock,17. Beretta/Sims/REX/Shutterstock, 18. Rob Cable/REX/Shutterstock, 19. Dave Hogan/Getty Images, 20-21. REX/Shutterstock, 23. Beretta/Sims/REX/Shutterstock, 24-25. Jonathan Short/AP/REX/Shutterstock, 25b. Mike Marsland/Getty Images, 27. Mat Hayward/Getty Images, 28. Kevin Mazur/Fox/WireImage/Getty Images, 29. David Krieger/Bauer-Griffin/GC Images, 30-31. Kevin Winter/Getty Images, 32l. Steve Granitz/WireImage/Getty Images, 32r. Dave M. Benett/Getty Images, 34-35. Richard Young/REX/Shutterstock, 36. Dave J Hogan/Getty Images, 37. Kim Raff/Getty Images for Sundance Film Festival, 38-39. David M. Benett/Dave Benett/Getty Images for Love Magazine & miu miu, 40-41. Yui Mok - WPA Pool /Getty Images, 42. David Fisher/REX/Shutterstock, 44-45. Jeff Kravitz/FilmMagic/Getty Images, 46-47. Matt Baron/BEI/REX/Shutterstock, 49. Kristina Bumphrey/StarPix/REX/Shutterstock, 50-51. PictureGroup/REX/Shutterstock, 52. Scott Barbour/Getty Images, 54-55. Kevin Mazur/WireImage/Getty Images, 56. Kevin Kane/Getty Images for Jingle Ball 2012, 57. Don Arnold/WireImage/Getty Images, 58-60. Dave J Hogan/Getty Images, 61. Ian Gavan/Getty Images for Sony Pictures, 62. Richard Young/REX/Shutterstock, 63. Kevin Winter/Getty Images, 64-65. IBL/REX/Shutterstock, 66. Willi Schneider/REX/Shutterstock, 68-69. Ryan Pierse/Getty Images, 70-71. IBL/REX/Shutterstock, 72. Steve Granitz/WireImage/Getty Images, 73. Most Wanted/REX/Shutterstock, 74-75. Joseph Okpako/FilmMagic/Getty Images, 76-77. Kevin Winter/Getty Images for iHeartMedia, 78-79. David Fisher/REX/Shutterstock, 80. Steve Jennings/WireImage/Getty Images, 81. Dave J Hogan/Dave J Hogan/Getty Images, 82. Eamonn M. McCormack/Getty Images, 83. Justin Tallis/AFP/Getty Images, 84. Daniel DeSlover/REX/Shutterstock, 85. Getty Images, 86-87. David Fisher/REX/Shutterstock, 89. Mark Davis/DCNYRE2016/Getty Images for dcp, 90. Jason Merritt/Getty Images, 92l. Mark Davis/DCNYRE2016/Getty Images for dcp, 92r. Francois Lo Presti/AFP/Getty Images, 93. Neil Mockford/GC Images, 94-95. Jason Merritt/Getty Images for iHeartMedia, 96. Martin Karius/REX/Shutterstock, 97. Emma McIntyre/Getty Images for SiriusXM, 98-99. REX/Shutterstock,100. Karwai Tang/WireImage/Getty Images,101. SMXRF/Star Max/GC Images/Getty Images, 102-103. Jeff Kravitz/FilmMagic for Sony Music/Getty Images, 104. Dave J Hogan/Dave J Hogan/Getty Images, 106-107. Eamonn M. McCormack - WPA Pool/Getty Images, 108-109. Dimitrios Kambouris/Getty Images for iHeart Media, 110. Francois Lo Presti/AFP/Getty Images, 112—113. John Lamparski/WireImage/Getty Images, 114-115. Rich Fury/Getty Images for iHeartMedia, 116. Steve Jennings/Getty Images for Sony Music, 118. Steve Jennings/Getty Images for Sony Music, 119. Kevin Winter/Getty Images for CBS RADIO, 120-121. Kevin Mazur/Getty Images for Sony Music, 122-123. Kevin Mazur/Getty Images for Sony Music, 124-125. Rich Fury/Getty Images for iHeartMedia, 127. Gary Gershoff/Getty Images, 128. Emma McIntyre/Getty Images for SiriusXM, 129. Ian Lawrence/GC Images, 130-131. Timothy Norris/WireImage for The Recording Academy, 132. Kevin Winter/Getty Images for CBS RADIO, 135. Laurent Viteur/WireImage/Getty Images, 137. Samir Hussein/WireImage/Getty Images, 138-139. Warner Bros/Kobal/REX/Shutterstock, 141. Dimitrios Kambouris/Getty Images for iHeart Media, 142. Steve Jennings/Getty Images for Sony Music, 145. JM Enternational/Shutterstock, 146. Don Arnold/WireImage, 148. Richard Young/Shutterstock, 149. Kevin Mazur/Getty Images for Harry Styles, 150-151. Stephen Lovekin/Shutterstock, 152. David Fisher/Shutterstock, 153. Barry King/Alamy Stock Photo, 154. Kevin Winter/Getty Images for The Recording Academy, 156. Kevin Mazur/Getty Images for Harry Styles, 157. Theo Wargo/Getty Images for Harry Styles, 159. © Walt Disney Studios Motion Pictures / © Marvel Studios / Courtesy Everett Collection, 161. Ron Smits/London Entertainment/Shutterstock, 162. Kevin Mazur/Getty Images for Spotify, 164. Simon Dack/Alamy Live News, 166. PA Images/Alamy Stock Photo, 167. Niyi Fote/TheNEWS2 via ZUMA Press Wire/Shutterstock, 169. Kevin Mazur/Getty Images for Harry Styles, 170. MediaPunch/Shutterstock, 171. Barry King/Alamy Stock Photo, 172-173. Ian West/PA Images/Alamy Stock Photo, 175. Jo Hale/Redferns.

Every effort has been made to acknowledge correctly and contact the source and/or copyright holder of each picture and Welbeck Publishing Limited apologises for any unintentional errors or omissions, which will be corrected in future editions of this book.

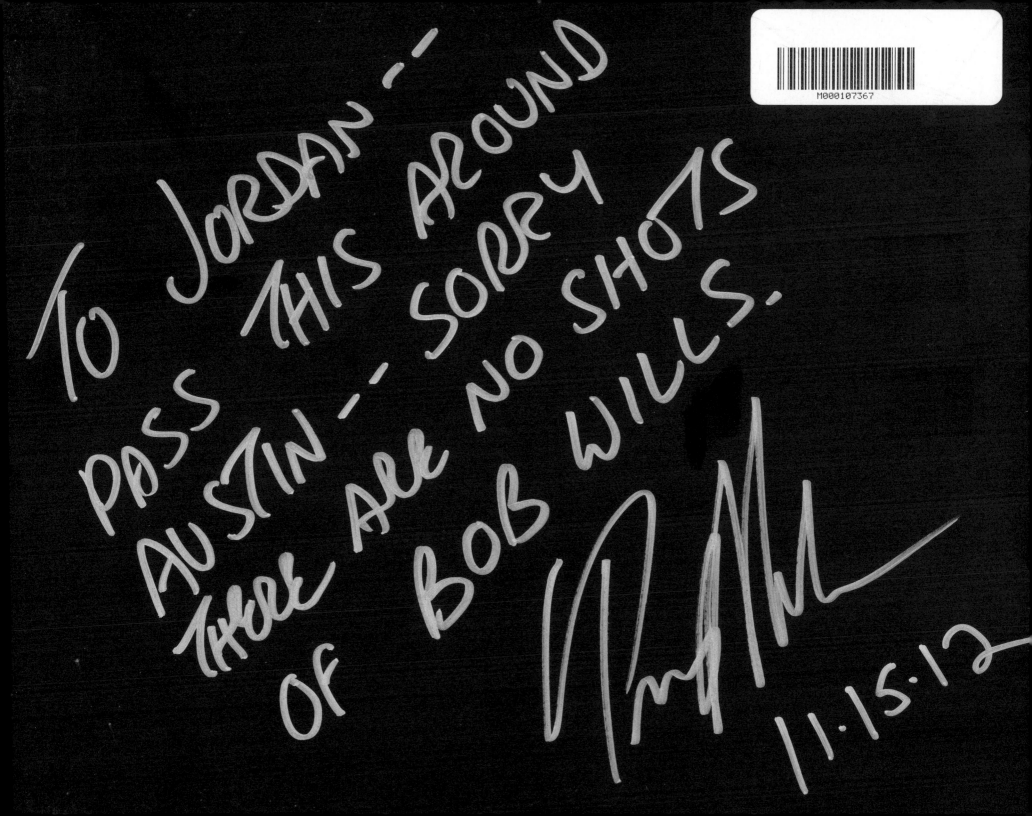

# IN THE BELLY OF THE BLUES

## Chicago to Boston to L.A. 1969 to 1983.  A Memoir.

## Words and Photos by Terry Abrahamson

Above from left: Taj Mahal, Pinetop Perkins, James Cotton

Rolling Fork Publishers
Chicago
rfpublishers@aol.com

© 2012 Terry Abrahamson

All rights reserved.

Library of Congress Control Number:  2012902810

ISBN: 978-0-578-10211-5


PRINTED IN CHINA

**John Lee Hooker** and **Koko Taylor**. The Rhode Island Blues Festival 1975

# A Note About These Photos

In 2002, music historian Robert Gordon called me from Memphis. He was doing a biography of Muddy Waters and was looking for photos, and got my name from Steady Rollin' Bob Margolin and even steadier rollin' Ted Kurland.  Yes, I had known Muddy - written songs with him, travelled with him and took a lot of photos of him and the others on these pages.

For nearly 30 years, they sat in a box in my closet: dusty negatives and slides, crumpled contact sheets and dog-eared prints - never intended for anything more than personal memories of some magical times. If I knew then what I know now, I'd have kept them in better shape.  I also would've taken my camera the night Dylan brought Victoria Spivey to see Muddy at The Bottom Line.  But when Robert found some of my shots usable, and they somehow made their way to the Rock and Roll Hall of Fame,  I figured someone else might enjoy them as well.

So here they are, cleaned up as best as I could get em. Sometimes blurry, sometimes dusty - and always loving - memories; not by a professional photographer, just by a fan and a friend who happened to have a camera in the right place at the right time.  As if these guys needed my help to live forever!

# When I First Met the Blues

**Howlin' Wolf.** Joe's Place, Cambridge 1974

Even growing up on the West Side of Chicago, I somehow made it to 18 knowing nothing about the Blues. I knew so much nothing that what lured my pal Abe Trieger and I to the Quiet Knight to see Howlin' Wolf was the chance to hear some guy who we'd heard was gonna perform what we had always thought of as a Rolling Stones song, *Little Red Rooster*.

Yeah, I knew so much nothing that when we got to the almost-empty club and were seated behind a rope in the under-21 section, I figured the six old Black guys huddled around one of the ringside tables in their white three dollar shortsleeeved shirts were the janitors. In fact, I would've bet the three-fifty cover charge that one of em was the guy in the Maintenance Crew photo in my 1968 Amundsen High School yearbook.

After all, I'd seen The Beatles in *A Hard Days Night*, and The Yardbirds on *Shindig* and Blood, Sweat and Tears at the Kinetic Playground. I knew what musicians looked like. These guys weren't it.

Then, with all the fanfare of a mechanic giving you the carburetor estimate, the p.a. proclaimed "Ladies and Gentlemen, The Howlin' Wolf Band." And those old guys moved from that table to their instruments about as slow as slow could go. You'd have moved slow too if you were dragging Charlie Patton and Son House and Robert Johnson up there with you.

Howlin' Wolf was big and Black and primitive and scary and like nothing I'd ever seen, illuminating the roots of all the music I'd ever loved: the Yardbirds, Cream, Mountain, Jimi Hendrix, Led Zeppelin and the Stones.

Abe and I spent most of the next hundred weekends six blocks away, seated on the floor of Alice's, a coffeehouse, at the feet of Wolf, Muddy Waters, Otis Rush: the Gods of Rock and Roll. And, in Alice's cramped quarters, we shared their backstage bathroom. That's how I met Muddy. For 13 years, from Chicago to Boston and back, our friendship grew. I cooked and drove for him, did his champagne runs, and took a lot of pictures.

This book is for Muddy Waters, Howlin' Wolf, not-totally Blind Jim Brewer, Jack Bruce, Ted "Unk in Funk" Kurland, Abe, Mike Salisbury, Rick Nowels... and dedicated to the ones I love: Vicki, Joe, Sam and Jake

# Alice's 1969-1971

You sat on the floor at Alice's: a room 20 feet wide with a two-foot high stage. We'd get there at 7 for the 9:30 set, and as the floor filled up behind us, the only reachable bathroom was backstage. These shots - taken with a Kodak Instamatic and a flashcube - were the first I ever took of Muddy Waters. The crutch behind drummer Willie Smith marks this as one of Muddy's first shows after surviving a near-fatal pelvis-crushing car crash. The bottle of Piper Heidseick champagne was as much a part of Muddy as his Fender Telecaster.

The clutched fist on the right tells me he was wrapping up *Long Distance Call, Five Long Years, Nineteen Years Old* or *Hoochie Coochie Man*. Those were the ones you paid to see. A whole $2.00; the deal of a lifetime. Of course, you could see Styx at Alice's every Tuesday for fifty cents.

3

Referring to Muddy in the song *Bio,* Chuck Berry says "It was he who showed me the way." Mick and Keith took their band's name from Muddy's song *Rolling Stone.* In 1964, upon landing in New York, Paul McCartney proclaimed "I'd like to see Muddy Waters." Muddy's recording of Willie Dixon's *You Need Love* was adapted by Led Zeppelin into *Whole Lotta Love,* generally regarded as one of the great rock songs of all time.

At Alice's, you got to see Muddy shake his jigsaw puzzle pelvis, and twitch and contort his elastic face as he wailed out the songs that Chuck Berry hitchhiked to Chicago to hear, long before Muddy had to wail them over the espresso machine hiss and the rumble of the Howard-Englewood el train.

**Pee Wee Madison** is on guitar. Muddy's attorney **Jay B. Ross** is on the floor. **Bob Koester** of Delmark Records is standing.

# The Orange and Blue Gets the Blues

In the late 60's and early 70's, the University of Illinois' flying saucer-like sports arena was always rocking to a steady stream of shows that featured the biggest names in music, including the Rolling Stones, Jethro Tull, Jefferson Airplane and the Temptations. But until the 1970 emergence in Champaign of Bluespower, a music co-operative to which I belonged, this perennial stop on the road from Mississippi to Chicago was strangely Blues-less.

Bluespower produced and financed on-campus shows featuring Hound Dog Taylor, Harmonica Frank Floyd and Alice's regular, not-totally Blind (read on) Jim Brewer. Following the resuscitation of his career by Leon Russell and Don Nix, Memphis' Furry Lewis, pictured above, paid us a visit in 1971.

# Payin' My Dues with B.B. King

It was the summer of 1971. And even though Abe and I had to wear ties and jackets to get through the door of Mr. Kelly's - Rush Street's swankiest nightclub - and even though his horn-backed Blues and snappy tux seemed a little further removed from Mississippi than the primitive brooding of Muddy and Wolf, when B.B. King tore up the house with *Don't Answer the Door* or *Sweet Sixteen*, the self-proclaimed "King of the Blues" was as real - and as Blue -as it could get.

Huey Thinks He's Got The Blues. But Tonight, The Blues Get Huey.

A Terry Abrahamson Film
**HOW BLUE CAN YOU GET?**
BLUE MOVIES ENTERTAINMENT presents
A TERRY ABRAHAMSON FILM HOW BLUE CAN YOU GET?
director of photography RON BELL editor ELENA MAGANINI
music by WILLIE DIXON and TERRY ABRAHAMSON
produced by PHILIP KOCH
written and directed by TERRY ABRAHAMSON
featuring the music of: MUDDY WATERS, WILLIE DIXON, HOWLIN' WOLF & KOKO TAYLOR

©1991 BLUE MOVIES ENTERTAINMENT ALL RIGHTS RESERVED

Ten years later, living in San Francisco, I opted for the Bluesiest vanity plate money could buy, and penned what I believed to be the obvious title cut on the album this can't-miss cover art would inspire: *License to Sing the Blues.*

Months later, with license plate and demo tape in one hand, and a borrowed state-of-the-art boombox in the other, I talked my way past the stage door and into B.B.'s dressing room at the Circle Star Theater in San Carlos. Initially disinterested, his ears perked up from the first note, and B.B. summoned his band, pointing at the speakers, proclaiming "That's the one; the one I been looking for." As my two-packs-of-Luckys-and-half-a-pint-of-gin demo vocal rasped on, I swooned with every affirmation of "That's the one!" echoed by B.B., his band and the two women on his ample lap. . When the song ended, B.B. clutched my wrist and asked "How much you want for this box?"

"What about the song?," I managed with a Mississippi-sized lump forming in my throat. "Oh, it's alright," he replied, "but how much for the box? I been lookin' for a box like this for*ever!*" When I produced the license plate, suggesting its cover art potential, the road manager was sure I'd stolen it off their bus in Tennessee. I escaped with the box, the license plate and a story I turned into a 1991 short film that won some awards, made it to HBO...and still hurts.

from CHICAGO...

## BLIND JIM BREWER

"The greatest folk-blues
guitarist in Chicago"

Flyer for the 1973
New England Tour

bookings:
music unlimited associates
42 Marlborough Street, Boston, Massachusetts 02115
617-536-2950

# Not-Totally-Blind Jim Brewer

I *thought* he was blind.
All those nights at Alice's when he was led to the stage, opening for Muddy and Wolf.  At the University of Illinois, when he was led to the dressing room, to the stage and to the hotel. And in September of 1973, after I'd moved to Boston to partner up with Ted Kurland booking Chicago Blues acts, when I had to drive 220 miles to pick him up in New York City for his New England tour because he wouldn't be able to switch trains to get up to Boston.

So I double-parked in front of Penn Station and rushed down to meet old friend and new client, Blind Jim Brewer. But as we emerged onto Eighth Avenue, the man for whom I'd just secured five weeks of work performing as a sightless Blues singer cast a milky eye on the curb 50 yards away and announced "Oh, you still gots that red car."

"Oh, I ain't *totally* blind. I just gots these cataracks. But, you know, that ain't how ya do it in show binness, so I just kinda let folks like you figure I'm blind and say what you want and if it come up, I just play dumb." That's how he explained it on the way back to Boston during one of our many McStops to sate his ravenous appetite.

For several weeks, not-totally-Blind Jim Brewer shared my bedroom. I got the floor. And from Boston to Buffalo, he delivered the authentic country Blues, sprinkled with a little gospel. And he delivered every night, whether performing alone, or headlining the bill as part of a mini-acoustic Blues festival that also featured  a 22 year old kid named George.
A White kid from Delaware.
An unknown.
At least for a little while longer.

Vermont 1973

The Hideaway, Granby, MA 1973

Not-totally-Blind Jim got through his tour inspite of some physical and emotional hardships. Prior to heading East, Jim had been attacked by a hammer-wielding intruder in his West Side apartment, and was left with some badly damaged fingers.

He also suffered from intermittent bouts of homesickness and, on more than one occasion, got a little weepy onstage. Fortunately, the adoring crowds figured he was just feelin' the Blues.

Jim was as entertaining offstage as he was at the mike. Returning from one of our mini-festivals at Bridgewater State College, Jim, George and I were stopped by a Massachusetts State Trooper who told us we matched the description of three guys who had held up a gas station. As we stood, legs spread and palms flat against the hood of "that red car" waiting for the cop to call in our i.d.'s, Jim whispered our instructions: "When he come back, George, you kick out his headlights, and Terry, you push him into me and I'll choke him." We encouraged Jim to develop a Plan B.

Heading home from another gig, Jim fantasized aloud about a young lady in the college audience. "I'd surely like to plug into her." I was inspired:

> The men call me Jim,
> The women call me "Electric Man."
> When I plug into your socket,
> I'll charge you like no-one else can.

Jim's not-quite-blind eyes lit up "That's good shit boy. You oughta give that to Muddy Waters," which I did when Muddy came to Boston weeks later. Muddy's reaction: "That's good shit, boy. Write that down." He recorded and released *Electric Man* the following year.

# And then there was the night we booked George Thorogood to play two sets for ten bucks.

# And then we took a commission.

# And then he thanked us.

**George Thorogood.** Sandy's Concert Club, Beverly, MA September 1973.

To stage even a *mini* Blues Fest, you need a second act. To open for Jim Brewer, we used an even lesser-known musician Abe, Ted and I had stumbled upon weeks earlier on the night I moved to Boston.

It was on July 5, 1973 after a 21 hour drive from Chicago. We headed straight for Joe Spadafora's legendary Blues bar, Joe's Place. The hand-lettered sign indicated the act was Sonny Terry and Brownie McGhee, blind and crippled although neither chose to mine the perceived show biz gold in spotlighting their respective physical challenges.

The opening act was on. I mean he was *ON!!!*

He got more Rock and Roll out of an acoustic guitar, bottleneck and harmonica than most guys could ever dream of making with a band. Bo Diddley, Chuck Berry, John Lee Hooker and Howlin' Wolf; he had their autographs taped to his guitar and their spirits engraved in his soul. He said he didn't need to compose any originals; that all the great songs had already been written. And he made them sound great all over again.

The next day, Ted and I booked some Hound Dog Taylor shows at Sandy's Concert Club in Beverly, north of Boston. We realized this kid from Joe's Place would be the perfect opening act...if 1) we could find him, and 2) he'd play for $10 a night; Sandy wouldn't pay a dime more. The guy who answered the phone at Joe's said the kid's name was George Thorogood and he'd gone back to Delaware where he lived with his mom.

We found Mrs. Thorogood through directory assistance in Wilmington. George was there and yeah, he'd love to open for Hound Dog....provided the gigs didn't conflict with the schedule of his baseball team, which they did not. When George didn't have the trainfare back to Boston, Ted and I Western Unioned it to him. When he had no place to crash, we gave him our couch on Marlboro Street. When he had no place to practice all night, we gave him our bathroom...it had that nice echoey feel. Later on, when he had no money to buy an electric guitar, we helped him out. That's when he brought his childhood pals, Jeff and Ron, up to start a three piece band. He used to say "Three pieces are all you need. Just look at Hound Dog Taylor and the Houserockers."

11

# Dean Junior College

Franklin, Massachusetts 02038 / (617) 528-9100

Office of Student Affairs

October 3, 1973

Ms. Terry Abrahamson
Music Unlimited Associates
416 Marlboro Street
Boston, Mass. 02100

Dear Terry:

Last weekend, being the first time I have worked with you, I honestly must say we did all right; as a matter of fact, we did better than all right. Blind Jim Brewer, George Thorogood and Sunnyland Train were all incredible considering they were packed into one weekend, I guess you would say we had one incredible weekend.

I wish you much luck and success with all of them and I would be more than happy to recommend them to any schools that would be interested in booking them.

Warmest regards,

Wendy

Wendy A. Wolff
Director of Student Activities

WAW/em
Enc.

Jim and George did six or eight shows together that September. Sunnyland Train, also referenced in Wendy's letter, shows up later in this book in some Big Walter pix. Their name comes from an Elmore James song, which meant they were alright with George.

Blues was a big deal with college kids back then. And it was a good chance to get more exposure for Jim, who had spent most of his playing career behind an open case Sunday mornings on Chicago's Maxwell Street. Jim and I talked about a 1974 tour in which we'd drop "Blind" from the promo material, but in the end, he was too homesick to leave Chicago.

Once drummer Jeff Simon and bassist Ron Smith joined George in his new digs on Peaceable Street in Brighton in late 1973, George was focused on going electric. And though they were baseball fans, one of George Thorogood and the Delaware Destroyers' first recordings was a basketball song. The Official 1974 Boston Celtics Fight Song was written by Herb Feuerstein and me as a way to get free season tickets. We called it *Champs Again* because Coach Tom Heinsohn wouldn't let us call it "Heinsohn's Heroes." Artist credit went to The Boston Basketball Band because George wouldn't let us use his name either; he said he was going to be famous soon and didn't want his name on a novelty record. Fair enough.

Herb and I got our season tickets. The song was played at every Celtics home game and Bob Ryan did two articles on us in The Boston Globe. We had intentionally used players' names in the song so that the following year, a new roster would mean a new song. But it wasn't meant to be. By 1975, the Celtics had had enough Rock and Roll. And Rock and Roll couldn't get enough of George and the Destroyers.

MY HOUSE, NOT MY GUNS. **George Thorogood** and **Jim Brewer**. Newton, MA, September 1973.

# You may have Dandridge and Cornell Warner,

CHAMPS AGAIN
(H. Feuerstein, T. Abrahamson)

GRANOLA RECORDS
© 1974 GRANOLA RECORDS

GR3001A
45 R.P.M.
TIME: 2:04

recorded at:
INTERMEDIA
SOUND
Boston, Mass.
produced by:
D. B. Shrier
engineer:
Bob Stoughton

THE BOSTON
BASKETBALL BAND

publisher:
ALL-AMERICAN
MUSIC
(B.M.I.)

## ...but we got Nelson and he hits from the corner.

George Thorogood and Jeff Simon.
Joe's Place, Cambridge, MA 1973

# Big Muddy Rolls into Boston

**Muddy Waters.** Paul's Mall, Boston 1974

I hadn't seen Muddy in two years on the night I hurried down to Paul's Mall with the lyrics to *Electric Man* folded in my pocket. The difference between Muddy at Alice's in 1971 and Muddy in Boston in the Fall of 1973 was remarkable.

This was no sit-on-the-floor coffee house. Paul's Mall was the Mr. Kelly's of Boston. You drank liquor. You dressed nice...nicer, anyway. Chicago, being the home of the Blues, was a place where the Blues was too often taken for granted. In Boston, Muddy Waters and his fellow Bluesmen were treated like honored guests...like music royalty, by the music press, the guy who ran the FM rock station and the local music celebrities like Duke Robillard and the J Geils Band.

And most unlike Chicago, you didn't just show up backstage to hang with Muddy. There were actual dressing rooms with doors: one for the star, one for the band. And before you were allowed back, you had to talk to a guy.

**Muddy Waters.** Paul's Mall, Boston 1973

After ten minutes, Muddy's half-brother/road manager, Antra Bolton, aka "Bo," emerged. My "remember me?" smile was greeted with a grunt and a beckoning jerk of his head. Our reunion apparently meant a lot more to me than it did to Bo. Backstage, the plot thickened.

Muddy's afro was gone. He'd also acquired a gorgeous 22 year old "significant other (my term; definitely not Muddy's)," Karen Dagmar from Winnetka. Galpal? Travelling Companion? Personal Assistant? The exact nature of their relationship was never explained, although KD insists she'll "talk about it someday."

KD's fellow Winnetkans included Republican Illinois Senator Charles Percy and W. Clement Stone, major contributor to - and confidante of - Nixon and Reagan. But Muddy knew how to handle that Mayflower crowd; he just shot a little Blue in their blood.

KD, mind you, was not your father's Winnetka debutante. Her Blues pedigree had its roots in an extended relationship with guitarist, Lefty Dizz, a decent entertainer, but nobody's idea of Blues royalty. She felt the music and her energy lit up Muddy like a Christmas tree. Every night. Onstage and off.

Happy to have a homey (relatively speaking of course), KD became my instant sister, and Muddy, from there on, introduced me as his "White Son." His digging the lyrics to *Electric Man* went a long way toward confirming the match in our spiritual DNA. And no, I wasn't his only "White Son." But I was happy to share the title.

Muddy's professional fortunes had also received a long overdue shot in the arm with the arrival of new business manager, Scott Cameron. Scott placed Muddy with A-list booking agency Premier Talent, where he joined a client list that included Led Zeppelin and The Who. Scott also succeeded in extricating Muddy from his 20 year relationship with Chess Records, freeing him to sign with Johnny Winter's Blue Sky label of Columbia Records. At the age of 60, Muddy finally had a chance to play the same arenas as the super-stars who idolized him, and to enjoy some real financial security. Backstage, the champagne was flowing.

Over the next three years, Muddy, KD and I ended most of our nights together down the street from Paul's Mall at Ken's Pub. As I scribbled lyrics on cocktail napkins, we bounced song ideas back and forth. Three actually bounced onto Muddy Waters lp's. *Electric Man* was joined by my second Muddy song - what was to be the title track on his 1974 Chess album. Again, I owe it all to Ted Kurland. One night, as Ted and I joked around with our then-roommate, Jim Brewer, Ted praised Jim as being not just funky, but "the man who put the 'unk' in funk." We brought the title to Muddy, who ordered me to break out the cocktail napkins. Minutes later, Muddy had his album title and its title song. And *Unk in Funk* gave Ted and I a little bit of Blues immortality.

The photos on these pages of **Muddy** and **KD** were taken backstage at Paul's Mall in 1973 and 1974,

With his pelvis healed and three young White kids - KD and guitarists Bob Margolin and Hollywood Fats - revitalizing his life and his music, Muddy's onstage personna radiated a power and sensuality that had long been waiting to explode.

It was best typified by the reintroduction of what became his signature song, *Mannish Boy*. *That* became the song you waited to hear. *That* became his star turn in The Band's *The Last Waltz*. It rocked Lincoln Center. It shook Carnegie Hall. Like he asks in the song:
*"Ain't THAT a man?"*

# And Ain't That a *Band*!

Hollywood Fats, Paul's Mall, Boston, 1973.

Bob Margolin, Rhode Island Blues Fest, 1975

At 19, Hollywood Fats was already a veteran of the John Lee Hooker and Albert King bands when he joined Muddy months before the Fall night in 1973 when hometown guitar hero, Brookline's Bob Margolin was hired on at Paul's Mall. Fats, born Michael Mann in L.A., and 24-year old Margolin brought very different styles to Muddy's band. Fats went on to play with Canned Heat and The Blasters. Steady rollin' Bob rolled right onto the big screen with Muddy in *The Last Waltz*, and hasn't stopped rollin' since.

George "Mojo" Buford was best known for the trademark harmonica bandolero that hung from his shoulder. Joe "Pinetop" Perkins was Muddy's age and had to hang around even longer for his greatest success, sharing a Grammy with Willie Smith at the age of 97.

At the top left are **Mojo**, **Muddy** and **Willie**. Above are **Muddy** and **Pinetop**, both shots from Paul's Mall, 1974.

On the steps in 1975, backstage at NYC's Bottom Line are, clockwise from center: **Antra "Bo" Bolton**, road manager; bassist **Calvin "Fuzz" Jones**; guitarist **Luther "Guitar Junior" Johnson**, who replaced Fats and sang a juicy version of Chick Willis' "Stoop Down Baby;" drummer **Willie "Big Eyes" Smith**; and George **"Mojo" Buford**.

# Blue Stew

What do you make Muddy Waters for dinner? Well, I'd invited him, and he accepted and now I was stuck....but not really. Combining every naive preconception I could muster with every item on Bob the Chef's menu that I could remember, I threw a few chickens in a big pot, added every vegetable I could find that ended in "greens," and poured in enough barbecue and hot sauce to send Tums stock soaring to record heights. Just to cover my ass, I plied Muddy with enough champagne to ensure he'd be able to burp it all up before showtime.

As you can see, Muddy ate it...and never complained...at least not within earshot.

Survivors around the table, from upper left, included **Ted Kurland, KD, Muddy, his son Charles,** me and, blurred in the foreground, our roommate Jerard, who I think owned those guns that George and Jim were playing with.

# Joe Spadafora
# Reintroduces
# Howlin' Wolf

Joe Spadafora was his own anthology of urban legends. Starting with how his original Joe's Place - the one pictured on these pages and the one where we first saw George open for Sonny & Brownie *and* the one where Bruce Springsteen and Bonnie Raitt had kicked off their careers - had burnt to the ground. The stories continued through - as the Big Man swore to me on more than one occasion - the night Joe drove Clarence Clemons from Cambridge to New Jersey in his Cadillac in an unrelenting thunderstorm.... with the top down.

Just as legendary was Joe's love for the music. And four years after the Wolf had introduced me to the Blues, it was Joe Spadafora who ushered him to the stage with the impassioned intro he deserved.

While Wolf's health was already failing in 1974, he could still shake Joe's Place - anybody's place - down to the foundations, with a lot of help from bandleader Eddie Shaw and guitar god, Hubert Sumlin. Eddie played a rockin' tenor sax and was a master at warming up the crowd and the ladies. Hubert let his guitar do most of his sweet talking after losing his front teeth years earlier - allegedly in a run-in with the Wolf. Wolf's other colorful sidemen included generously scarred keyboardist Detroit Junior and bassist Chicken House Shorty whose horrifying limp would've ensured his immortality as the Ratso Rizzo of the Blues...had such a title existed.

**Hound Dog Taylor** and **Ted Harvey.**
Sandy's Concert Club, Beverly, MA 1971

# Hound Dog Taylor's Motel Room Chicken:

# Magic Fingers-Lickin' Good!

**Hound Dog,** Backstage at Paul's Mall 1974

Hound Dog Taylor was a tremendously entertaining Elmore James-style slide guitarist. We first met in 1971 when he headlined a show for Bluespower at the University of Illinois. That was around the time he had signed with Bruce Iglauer's fledgling Alligator Records label. He travelled with a guitar player, a drummer and a plug-in frying pan.

Hound Dog, Brewer Philips and Ted Harvey would roll into town, buy some chicken, break out the flour and pork-fat and fry it up in the motel room. Definitely a guy with an ornery side....there had even been a story about somebody in the band being shot in a workplace-related incident...I guess Hound Dog commandeering a pan of sizzling porkfat made me so nervous I never thought of snapping photos in the motel. Nor did I ever get a shot of his eleventh finger...or eleventh toe.

**Brewer Phillips**

**Ted Harvey**

**Hound Dog** and his band at Sandy's, Beverly, MA 1973

29

**Hound Dog Taylor, KD** and **Muddy Waters** backstage at Paul's Mall, 1974

**Ted Harvey** uses mouth-to-mouth resuscitation to revive a fan. 1974

In 1991, for my bio-short based on the B.B. King story, I needed extras and hired **Brewer Phillips** (left) and KD's old boyfriend **Lefty Dizz**.

# Big Walter Horton

Muddy's former sideman visited Paul's Mall in 1974, part of a steady stream of musicians who came to hang out and sit in.

**Big Walter Horton, Steve Brown** and **Bob Frank.**
Backstage at Paul's Mall 1974.

Steve Brown and Bob Frank had relocated from
Cleveland, joining hundreds of other musicians
in the hub of the Blues renaissance. On this night
backstage at Paul's Mall, they were fortunate
enough to get a lesson from one of the
old masters, Big Walter Horton.

We had all moved to Boston around the same
time, and I had gotten some gigs for their group,
The Nathaniel Graves Band. One night, they were
about to go onstage when they were informed
that their lead guitarist had quit the band. To
make a Bluesy situation even Bluesier, the depart-
ing guitarist's name was Nathaniel Graves.

By the second set, they were performing as Sunnyland Train, the name of an Elmore James song.

# Sideman Serenade

Another former sideman....and another Luther Johnson, to boot!...Luther "Snake" Johnson hit Paul's Mall in 1974. Luther "Snake" Johnson, while *not* to be confused with Luther "Guitar Junior" Johnson, *was* to be confused with his own alter ego, Luther "Georgia Boy" Johnson.

On the right, also at Paul's Mall, the pride of Westerly, Rhode Island, the great Duke Robillard, who, before going solo, fronted one of New England's most popular bands, Roomful of Blues.

# The James Cotton Band

In New England, Muddy's former harmonica player found the fame that had eluded him....that eluded *most* Blues musicians....in Chicago. Cotton's band had such a big following that when Muddy played Paul's Mall, it wasn't just Cotton sitting in; it was each bandmember sitting in, and all treated like celebrities. That band included Matt "Guitar" Murphy, who got famous playing guitar - and Aretha Franklin's movie husband - with The Blues Brothers.

Injecting a rare dose of tenor sax into Muddy's sound was Cotton's horn man, Chavis "Little Bo" Sheriff. Little Bo bore an uncanny resemblance to Muddy, although Muddy was never known to perform in silver-studded black leather.

# The White Otis Spann

Otis Spann, still another of Muddy's half-brothers, was the pianist on most of Muddy's most significant Chess recordings. Spann had died in 1970. While Muddy seemed perfectly content to soldier on with Pinetop Perkins inheriting the keys, when David Maxwell sat in, you could see that faraway glow in Muddy's eyes as he whispered "just like Spann."

Maxwell, pictured here at Paul's Mall in 1974, first crossed my radar with some work he'd done for Bonnie Raitt. He played with a lot of people,and was one of a stream of outstanding keyboardists who sat in with Muddy. But he always seemed to hold a special place in the Old Man's heart.

In the bottom photo, Maxwell plays along with Willie Smith, Mojo Buford and Calvin "Fuzz" Jones.

# But Not as White as Johnny Winter

In 1975, when Johnny Winter showed up to play with Muddy at New York's Bottom Line, it wasn't just as a fan or protege. It was as a recording executive who was about to change his idol's fortunes. Winter was largely responsible for Muddy's move from Chess Records to Columbia's Blue Sky label.

Muddy sold more records, had his profile elevated still closer to where it should've been all along, and recorded his final albums for the same label as his fellow Rock and Roll Hall of Fame inductees, Bob Dylan, Bruce Springsteen and Billy Joel.

Grammy-winning HARD AGAIN, Muddy's first album for Blue Sky, featured the song *Bus Driver*, the third song co-written by Muddy and I. It was the longest song on the album and featured Johnny and Bob Margolin on guitars, Pinetop on piano, Willie Smith on drums and James Cotton on harmonica.

**Johnny Winter,** backstage at The Bottom Line, NYC 1975.

# The 1975 Rhode Island Blues Festival

Koko Taylor

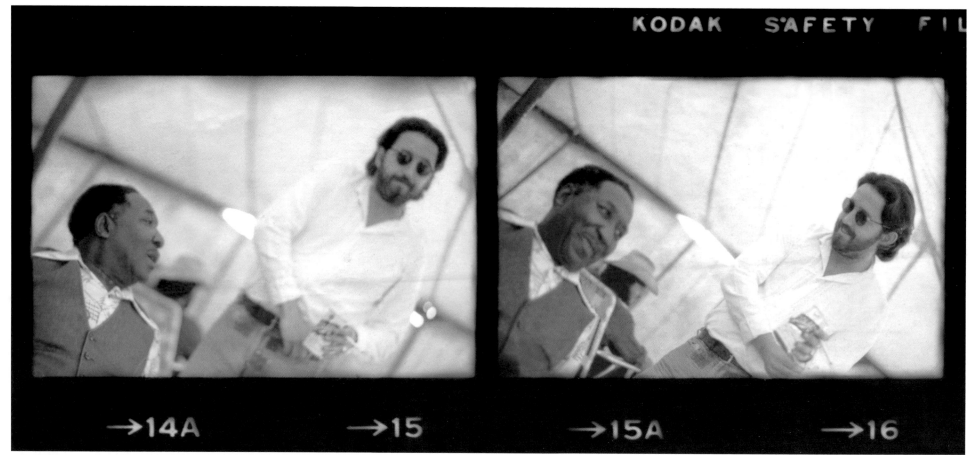

KODAK S'AFETY FIL

→14A  →15  →15A  →16

**Muddy Waters** and **Paul Butterfield**

Muddy, Freddie King, John Lee Hooker, Koko Taylor, Taj Mahal, Roomful of Blues, Paul Butterfield. One of the last opportunities to see so many big names together. And, as was usually the case with Muddy Waters, the interaction backstage was as memorable as the performances. And it all went down at that most Bluesy sounding of places, the Stepping Stone Ranch in Escoheag, Rhode Island.

**Koko Taylor** and **Freddie King**

Freddie King

**Freddie King** and **Muddy Waters** diggin' that dashboard shag.

Taj Mahal and Muddy Waters

Freddie King and Taj Mahal

John Lee Hooker

Koko Taylor

"Don't say nothin' boy,
but the Stones is
s'posed to show up."

The summer of '79. Muddy was back home, between sets at the Quiet Knight; a rare club gig these days for a guy who needed most of the energy once expended on a second set of songs for his last set of kids. His new wife (second from the left) Marva - aka Sunshine - had moved Mud to greener pastures: suburban Westmont.

As visitors filed in, Muddy corralled one guy in his 40's, then, nudging the napping toddler in his lap (see above), Muddy told his young son "Say hello to your brother."  Minutes later, Muddy's manager, Scott Cameron whispered something to Muddy, who disappeared, returning in a three piece suit.

**Muddy Waters, Scott Cameron, Willie Dixon**

Waiting for Muddy was Willie Dixon. Dixon had penned a major percentage of the many Blues and Rock and Roll classics resonating from the Chess years: *I Just Want to Make Love to You, I Can't Quit You Baby, Back Door Man, Hoochie Coochie Man*...to name a very few. The significance of his appearance on this night wasn't lost on Muddy; it was one of Dixon's first trips out since losing his leg to diabetes.

During a quiet exchange between Scott and Dixon, Muddy leaned close to my ear: "Don't say nothin' boy, but the Stones is s'posed to show up."

Clockwise from top: **Willie Dixon** framed by the silhouettes of Muddy and Ron Wood; **Mick Jagger** and Willie's daughter, **Shirley Dixon; Mick Jagger** and **Willie Dixon.** All backstage, the Quiet Knight, 1979.

Keith Richards and Ron Wood were the first ones to show up. Keith's entrance remains a memory. Still in the doorway, his eyes searched for, and locked on, Muddy. He tossed aside the cigarette dangling from his lower lip, crossed the room to the original Rollin' Stone, knelt at Muddy's feet and kissed his hand. Moments later, Mick Jagger and Charlie Watts arrived with Mick's girlfriend, Jerry Hall.

It had been 10 years since I'd first gone down to the Quiet Knight to see somebody named Howlin' Wolf do what I thought was a Rolling Stones song. Now, I was hanging out with the Stones and the guy who Little Red Rooster really belonged to: Willie Dixon. And the night was just getting started.

**Mick Jagger** and **Keith Richards** with a guy I have never been able to identify.

**Keith Richards** with **Willie Dixon** behind his right shoulder.

**Mick Jagger**

Ron Wood, Keith Richards and Charlie Watts

# "Where's my friends?"

Muddy began the second set by introducing Willie Dixon, who made it to the stage with a cane. After a few numbers, Willie took his seat, and there was some kind of announcement about anyone who thought they might have to leave should go now. These were pre-cellphone days and the great concern must've been about who would run to a pay phone to alert the press.

Then it got quiet, and Muddy looked around before shouting "Where's my friends? Mick! Charlie! Keith! Ronnie!" As the Rolling Stones took the stage, the room temperature of the Quiet Knight rose by maybe 30 degrees. For the next 35 minutes, Mick and his mates, supported by Bob Margolin and Pinetop Perkins, ran Muddy through *Mannish Boy, Got My Mojo Workin', Baby, Please Don't Go* and a few more Muddy Waters classics. And Muddy still remembered most of the lyrics.

Ron Wood, Muddy Waters, Mick Jagger and Keith Richards

WATERTOONS MUSIC
16 South Adams Street
Westmont, Illinois 60559

## STATEMENT OF ROYALTIES

SIX MONTHS ENDING December 31, 1979     FOR   Terry Abrahamson
2220 N. Sedgwick
Chicago, Illinois   60614

| COMPOSITION | COPIES | | MECHANICALS, ETC. | | TOTAL ROYALTY |
| --- | --- | --- | --- | --- | --- |
| | NUMBER SOLD | ROYALTY RATE | INCOME | ROYALTY RATE | |
| BUS DRIVER (With M. Morganfield) | | | | | |
| Domestic | | | 782 26 | 25% | 195 57 |
| Canada | | | 46 21 | 25% | 11 55 |
| United Kingdom | | | 66 45 | 25% | 16 61 |
| Denmark | | | 15 11 | 25% | 3 78 |
| Switzerland | | | 24 61 | 25% | 6 15 |
| ELECTRIC MAN (With A. Cooper) | | | | | |
| Germany | | | 10 68 | 25% | 2 67 |
| UNK IN FUNK (With A. Cooper, T. Kurland) | | | | | |
| Germany | | | 11 86 | 16 2/3% | 1 97 |
| TOTAL DUE | | | | | $238.30 |

*WHERE'S MY COMMISSION*

*Muddy Waters*

COMPOSITIONS NOT ENUMERATED ON STATEMENT
HAVE HAD NO SALES

# A Note from Muddy

The songs I wrote with Muddy (who periodically gave writer's credit to his granddaughter A. Cooper for reasons best left to lawyers) were published by Muddy's Watertoons Music.

Sometimes, Muddy would scribble notes on the statements he sent out with the checks. As Muddy taught himself to write fairly late in life, he was particularly proud of these notes...nearly as proud as I was to have them.

# Waist Deep in The Blues

In the early 1980's, while living in San Francisco, I wrote and produced commercials for Levis Jeans. Sharing my musical passions, the Levi Strauss execs were very supportive of the ads I produced with original music created for the Chambers Brothers and Chicago Blues diva, Valerie Wellington (*I Want a Man with the Blues*). The sessions were produced by Rick Nowels, with who I also co-wrote the Joan Jett song, *Just Lust*.

One such ad was created for John Lee Hooker: *Waist Deep in the Blues*. Figuring John Lee could replicate the reference groove I liked from his HOOKER 'N HEAT lp, we saw no need to hire another guitarist. But when John Lee showed up, and we discussed the track, he sighed and said he "couldn't play that thing no more."

As panic set in, the engineer at our Hollywood recording studio said he had the ideal guy in mind to play the old boogie riff we needed. We told him to make the call, and a short time later, in walked Hollywood Fats, Muddy Waters' old guitarist. Fats heard what we wanted, remembered it well, and nailed it on the first take.

Although it was cropped out of this photo, inspired by John Lee's bit in The Blues Brothers' movie, we miked his right foot as it tapped out the beat.

# Still Bluesy After All These Years

**Bob Margolin, Terry Abrahamson** and **Karen Dagmar "KD" Swift**
Evanston, IL   October 2011